# Lecture Notes in Artificial Intelligence    1612

Subseries of Lecture Notes in Computer Science
Edited by J. G. Carbonell and J. Siekmann

## Lecture Notes in Computer Science

Edited by G. Goos, J. Hartmanis and J. van Leeuwen

Y0-BYM-317

**Springer**
*Berlin*
*Heidelberg*
*New York*
*Barcelona*
*Hong Kong*
*London*
*Milan*
*Paris*
*Singapore*
*Tokyo*

Ralph Bergmann   Sean Breen
Mehmet Göker   Michel Manago   Stefan Wess

# Developing Industrial Case-Based Reasoning Applications

## The INRECA Methodology

 Springer

Authors

Ralph Bergmann
University of Kaiserslautern, Department of Computer Science
P.O. Box 3049, D-67653 Kaiserslautern, Germany
E-mail: bergmann@informatik.uni-kl.de

Sean Breen
IMS, Clara House, Glenageary Park, Co. Dublin, Ireland
E-mail: sbreen@imsgrp.com

Mehmet Göker
DaimlerChrysler AG, Forschung und Technologie 3
P.O. Box 2360, D-89013 Ulm, Germany
E-mail: mehmet.goeker@daimlerchrysler.com

Michel Manago
AcknoSoft, 15 rue Soufflot, F-75005 Paris, France
E-mail: manago@acknosoft.com

Stefan Wess
TECINNO GmbH, Sauerwiesen 2, D-67661 Kaiserslautern, Germany
E-mail: wess@tecinno.com

Cataloging-in-Publication data applied for

**Die Deutsche Bibliothek - CIP-Einheitsaufnahme**

**Developing industrial case based reasoning applications** : the INRECA
methodology / Ralph Bergmann .... - Berlin ; Heidelberg ; New York ;
Barcelona ; Hong Kong ; London ; Milan ; Paris ; Singapore ; Tokyo :
Springer, 1999
   (Lecture notes in computer science ; 1612 : Lecture notes in artificial
   intelligence)
   ISBN 3-540-66182-4

CR Subject Classification (1998): I.2, J.1, J.3

ISBN 3-540-66182-4 Springer-Verlag Berlin Heidelberg New York

© Springer-Verlag Berlin Heidelberg 1999
Printed in Germany

Typesetting: Camera-ready by author
SPIN 10705149    06/3142 – 5 4 3 2 1 0     Printed on acid-free paper

# Preface

## Getting Intelligently Closer to Customers:
## The Role of Case-Based Reasoning in 21st Century Business

**Wolfgang Martin, META Group**

As this century comes to a close, global competition is escalating into an uphill race among enterprises to capture and retain the most customers that generate the most profits. Historically, the "supply chain," which supports product development and marketing, was typically started — and ended — in the form of routine customer account and service data. Winners in the new century will be those organizations that successfully extend and incorporate newer and richer types, sources, and users of internal and external customer information and establish new channels for interaction. Customer centricity and intimacy will become the key differentiating factor of enterprises when there are no longer any differences in products or services. This is the situation in hyper-competitive, saturated, and global market places.

Customer centricity must address these key issues:

1. enabling the virtual corporation via linkage of enterprise resource planning/management (ERP/ERM) and supply chain planning/management (SCP/SCM) with customer relationship management (CRM), the new business process at the front office.
2. integrating, monitoring, and controlling customer-centric business processes via data warehouse, OLAP, and data mining,
3. delivering Web-enabled applications to provide e-business/e-commerce as a new channel to customers, thus starting a new generation of interactivity at the point of contact/sale.

This indicates and emphasizes the importance of information for building a 21st-century business. Information must be treated in the same way as any product of the virtual corporation, and in this sense, the supply chain for the product information can be called an "Information Supply Chain." This value chain describing the logistics of information has to act according to the supply chain paradigm:

*Deliver the right information to the right information consumer in the right location just in time and create an added value.*

Issues leading to the creation of these virtual corporations include:

- purchasing control shifting from vendor push to customer pull,
- ability of enterprises to succeed in offering products/services as defined by individual customers,
- excellence at three vital customer touch-points to implement winning strategies: marketing, sales, and service,
- ability to go to market with increasing frequency and accuracy.

Beyond the insular single-enterprise information supply chain lies the architectural challenges of e-commerce, direct customer access to corporate data assets, and business-to-business application connectivity. As the number of such inter-enterprise users increases, so too must the level of self-service information content in the application interface increase, because of the inability to train inter-corporate users on application nuances. Web browsers and next-generation user interfaces such as information portals offer the promise of common graphical user interface (GUI) usage and content guidelines. Through to 2001, most application package vendors will focus on function and technology underpinnings, leaving users to assume the burden of creating and maintaining API engines or data service interfaces and architectural integration of application packages.

## Rise of the Virtual Corporation

**Drivers/Enablers**

- new global economics
- lifetime view of most profitable customer segments
- shared data across all customer touch-points
- multiple service contracts and many peers
- Internet at center stage

**Barriers/Obstacles**

- dystopia may occur as islands of automation proliferate
- architectural impedance mismatch between application packages
- organizational, cultural, and political roadblocks
- lack of a shared, service-oriented business model

To support the coalescence of an information supply chain, the resulting "Information Logistics" discipline – composed of a data warehouse architecture, methodology, and deployment processes – becomes mission-critical to the ongoing maintenance and evolution of the business-driven and customer-centric data warehouse. Clearly, customer relationship management (CRM) applications – linking the major customer touch-points within the supply chain – will be the ultimate in data warehouse applications as the boundaries among IT, marketing, and customers diminish.

Customer intelligence is at the heart of CRM solutions. It is provided by an analytical application that is part of the information supply chain enabling the monitoring and controlling of the CRM process via a closed-loop system approach. In this sense, it provides an intelligent solution to understanding and modeling the dynamics and behavior of the customer and to delivering the knowledge to initiate action (i.e., how to optimally address customer needs via the CRM process). This intelligence is provided by data mining technologies like neural networks, genetic algorithms, fuzzy logic, and Case-Based Reasoning (CBR). It is thus fair to say that closed-loop CRM systems will turn out to be the "killer applications" for all flavors of data mining.

Data-mining-enabled CRM packages that facilitate integrated closed-loop CRM process support to address the "customer-centricity" paradigm are coming to market now. These integrated packages will also integrate third-party data sources from the Web to open the deluge of web click-stream data for customer intelligence. By 1999/2000, today's batch-oriented, remote-type usage of data mining for customer intelligence will be complemented by real-time data mining for tasks like customer scoring and segmenting, and data and information filtering. By then, CBR and text mining will be another complement to traditional data mining and will greatly enhance the scope of customer intelligence. By 2000/01, intelligent software agents will have created the next generation of data-mining technologies and be providing transparent, real-time customer intelligence technology. By 2001/02, the agents will enable "mining" of traditional structured data as well as multimedia types of unstructured data (text, voice, image, and so on). CBR technologies will be key to building these intelligent software agents.

Because of the increasing number of data-mining technologies and solutions, understanding and implementing the data-mining process are essential. A "data analysis framework" (DAF) provides the methodology and the framework for a state-of-the-art, semi-automated data-mining process linking data mining to the CRM solution. A DAF is an iterative, business-driven process encompassing a set of data-mining methods and tools. In general, a DAF is deployed that is based on integrated data warehouse/data-mining infrastructure and supported by the leading system integrators. This drives the delivery of horizontal and vertical applications in the domain of customer intelligence. The INRECA CBR methodology, described in this book, provides a DAF for CBR and is now coming to market. This indicates the maturity of CBR technologies and strengthens the role of CBR as a key technology for customer intelligence.

March 1999

# Table of Contents

**About this Book** ................................................................................. 1

**Acknowledgments** ............................................................................. 5

**Part I :   Smarter Business with Case-Based
            Decision Support** ...................................................... 7

**1. Making Smarter Business Decisions in Less Time** ..................... 9

    1.1   Why Case-Based Decision Support? .................................... 10
    1.2   What Is Case-Based Decision Support? ............................... 11
        1.2.1   Case-Based Reasoning ............................................ 11
        1.2.2   Knowledge Discovery and Data Mining .................. 13
    1.3   Successful Applications of Case-Based Decision Support ..... 14
        1.3.1   Management of Industrial Knowledge ..................... 14
        1.3.2   Sales Support .......................................................... 14
        1.3.3   Reliability Analysis ................................................ 14
        1.3.4   Technical Support ................................................... 15
    1.4   Benefits of Case-Based Decision Support ........................... 15
    1.5   Case-Based Decision Support and Alternative Techniques ... 15
        1.5.1   Statistics ................................................................. 16
        1.5.2   Expert Systems ....................................................... 16
        1.5.3   Databases ................................................................ 17
    1.6   Development Process and Case Collection .......................... 17
    1.7   How Are Cases Retrieved? ................................................. 18
    1.8   How Are Cases Represented? ............................................. 19

**2. Case-Based Reasoning Approaches** ........................................... 21

    2.1   The Textual CBR Approach ............................................... 22
    2.2   The Conversational CBR Approach .................................... 23
    2.3   The Structural CBR Approach ........................................... 25

2.4   Comparing the Different Approaches ........................................28
2.5   Effort Required for the Different Approaches .........................31
2.6   Overall Assessment of the Different CBR Approaches ..........33

## 3. Selected Applications of the Structural Case-Based Reasoning Approach..........................................................35

3.1   HOMER: A Case-Based CAD/CAM Help-Desk Support Tool.............36
    3.1.1   DaimlerChrysler's Motivation ......................................36
    3.1.2   Initial Situation at the CAD/CAM Help-Desk ...............36
    3.1.3   Project Goals and Benefits..........................................38
    3.1.4   Knowledge Representation ..........................................39
    3.1.5   The HOMER System ....................................................40
    3.1.6   Users and Roles ..........................................................44
    3.1.7   Lessons Learned .........................................................44
    3.1.8   Results Achieved .........................................................45
    3.1.9   Summary......................................................................46
3.2   A Case-Based Product Catalog of Operational Amplifiers....................47
    3.2.1   The Application Development Process.........................48
    3.2.2   Benefit Analysis..........................................................48
    3.2.3   Similarity Functions Used in the Application .............49
    3.2.4   How the Software Works..............................................50
    3.2.5   Status of the Application.............................................54
3.3   Case-Based Maintenance Support for TGV Trains..............................55
    3.3.1   TGV's Environment ....................................................55
    3.3.2   A Hierarchy of Data Models and Case Bases .............55
    3.3.3   Technical Approach for Diagnosis...............................57
    3.3.4   Example of the System in Action.................................58
    3.3.5   Integration into the End-User Environment .................59
    3.3.6   Status of the Application..............................................61

## Part II:   Developing Case-Based Application with the INRECA Methodology .....................................63

## 4. Practical Guidelines for Developing Case-Based Reasoning Applications .............................................................65

4.1   Define Your Measures of Success ............................................66
4.2   Orient Your Customers ............................................................67
4.3   Get the Big Picture...................................................................68
4.4   Think About Maintenance.........................................................69
4.5   Welcome Feedback and Testing ...............................................70
4.6   Measure the Success ...............................................................71

4.7    Direct Access for the Customer ........................................................... 72
4.8    Market Your Success .......................................................................... 73
4.9    Expand the Scope ................................................................................ 74

## 5.  Professional Case-Based Reasoning Application Development ........................................................................................ 77

5.1    Why Do You Need the INRECA Methodology? .................................. 78
       5.1.1   How You Benefit from a Methodology ...................................... 78
       5.1.2   What the INRECA Methodology Can Do for You .................... 78
       5.1.3   Ensuring High-Quality Software ................................................ 79
5.2    Foundations from Software Engineering .............................................. 79
       5.2.1   The Experience Factory and the Quality Improvement Paradigm ......... 80
       5.2.2   Software Process Modeling ........................................................ 82
5.3.   The CBR Experience Base ................................................................... 84
       5.3.1   Experience Captured in Software Process Models .................... 85
       5.3.2   Experience on Different Levels of Abstraction .......................... 85
5.4    How to Apply the INRECA Methodology to New Projects .................. 86
5.5    Capturing Your Own CBR Experience ................................................. 88
5.6    The INRECA Methodology and Quality Standards .............................. 90

## 6.  Documenting Case-Based Reasoning Development Experience ...................................................................................... 91

6.1    Into the Details of Processes, Products, and Methods .......................... 92
       6.1.1   Software Processes: The Basic Activities .................................. 92
       6.1.2   Technical, Organizational, and Managerial Processes .............. 93
       6.1.3   How Processes Interact .............................................................. 93
       6.1.4   Combining Processes to Process Models ................................... 95
6.2    Generic and Specific Descriptions ....................................................... 95
       6.2.1   Generic Descriptions .................................................................. 96
       6.2.2   Specific Descriptions ................................................................. 96
6.3    Detailed Description of Process Models ............................................... 97
       6.3.1   Process Description Sheets ......................................................... 98
       6.3.2   Product Description Sheets ....................................................... 100
       6.3.3   Simple Method Description Sheets ........................................... 100
       6.3.4   Complex Method Description Sheets ........................................ 103
6.4    Tool Support for Documenting the Experience ................................... 104
       6.4.1   Rationale for Selecting Visio ................................................... 105
       6.4.2   Standard Recursive Structure ................................................... 105
       6.4.3   Managing Several Recipes and Projects ................................... 106
       6.4.4   HTML Publication ..................................................................... 106

# Part III:   Using the Methodology in Different Domains ................................................................. 107

## 7. Developing Case-Based Help-Desk Support Systems for Complex Technical Equipment ........................................ 109

7.1   Characteristics of Case-Based Help-Desk Support Systems ................ 110
7.2   Development and Use of Case-Based Help-Desk Support Systems
      for Complex Technical Equipment ...................................................... 111
      7.2.1   Process Types ........................................................................ 111
      7.2.2   Managerial Processes During System Development ........................... 111
      7.2.3   Organizational Processes During System Development ..................... 113
      7.2.4   Technical Processes During System Development ............................. 115
7.3   Using the System ............................................................................. 119
      7.3.1   Managerial Processes During System Use ......................................... 119
      7.3.2   Organizational Processes During System Use ................................... 120
      7.3.3   Technical Processes During System Use ........................................... 120
7.4   Process Model for a Help-Desk Project ............................................... 123
7.5   Impact of the Methodology in Developing and Using Help-Desk
      Support Systems ............................................................................... 127
      7.5.1   Impact of the Methodology During Project Definition ...................... 129
      7.5.2   Impact of the Methodology During System Development ................. 129
      7.5.3   Impact of the Methodology During System Use ............................... 130
7.6   Conclusion ...................................................................................... 130

## 8. Developing Intelligent Catalog Search Applications .............. 133

8.1   Characteristics of an Intelligent Catalog Search Project ...................... 134
8.2   Vertical Platform for Catalog Search ................................................. 135
      8.2.1   Case Structure and Domain Model ................................................. 136
      8.2.2   Defining Similarity ..................................................................... 136
      8.2.3   Customer Dialogs ....................................................................... 137
      8.2.4   Integration with Product Database ................................................. 137
      8.2.5   Web Interface ............................................................................. 138
8.3   Process Model for Catalog Search ..................................................... 139
      8.3.1   Requirements Acquisition ............................................................ 139
      8.3.2   Case Base Development ............................................................... 141
      8.3.3   GUI Development ........................................................................ 142
      8.3.4   Implement CBR Engine ............................................................... 143
      8.3.5   Integrate CBR and GUI ............................................................... 143
8.4   Benefits of the Methodology ............................................................. 144

## 9. Developing Maintenance Applications .......................................... 147

9.1    Characteristics of a Maintenance Application for Complex
       Technical Equipment ...................................................................... 148
       9.1.1   Typical Input and Output ................................................... 148
       9.1.2   Technical Characteristics .................................................. 149
9.2    Vertical Platform for Maintenance ................................................ 150
       9.2.1   Domain Model: The Hierarchical Approach ........................ 151
       9.2.2   Case Acquisition Process ................................................... 152
9.3    Impact of the Methodology in a Maintenance Application of
       Complex Technical Equipment ....................................................... 154
       9.3.1   Productivity for Building a Diagnostic Support Application .............. 155
       9.3.2   Quality of the Results Obtained .......................................... 155
       9.3.3   Improved Communication .................................................. 156
       9.3.4   Managing Decision Making ................................................ 156

## A. Compilation of INRECA Methodology Applications ............. 159

A.1    ALSTOM – Improving Train Availability to Optimize Operating
       Cost ............................................................................................... 159
A.2    ANALOG DEVICES – Sales Support for Integrated Circuits ............. 160
A.3    ANSALDO – Maintaining the Metro in Naples .............................. 161
A.4    CENTRE NATIONAL D'ETUDES SPATIALES – Optimizing
       the Reliability of Ariane ................................................................ 162
A.5    DAIMLERCHRYSLER – The Intelligent Hotline ............................ 163
A.6    GICEP ELECTRONIQUE – Diagnostic Help for Circuit Boards
       Used in Halogen Stove-Tops ........................................................... 164
A.7    IRSA – Expertise Knowledge-Base ................................................ 164
A.8    LEGRAND – Rapid Cost Estimation for Plastic Parts Production ....... 165
A.9    MET-ERICSSON – Analyzing Telecommunication Cards and
       Electronic System Test Data ........................................................... 166
A.10   MÜRITZ ONLINE – Tourist Information on the Internet .................... 168
A.11   ODENSE STEEL SHIPYARD – Improving Performances of Ship
       Welding Robots .............................................................................. 168
A.12   SEPRO ROBOTIQUE – Customer Support of Robots for the
       Plastics Industry ............................................................................ 169
A.13   SEXTANT AVIONIQUE – Troubleshooting Avionics for Airbus
       Airplanes ....................................................................................... 170
A.14   SIEMENS – SIMATIC Knowledge Manager .................................. 171
A.15   SNECMA SERVICES – Troubleshooting Boeing 737 Engines .......... 172
A.16   THE COMPENDIUM "PRECISION FROM RHINELAND-
       PALATINATE" – Product and Catalog on the Internet ...................... 173
A.17   WARTSILÄ NSD – Extending Marine Engine Life Cycles and
       Easing their Maintenance ............................................................... 174

**Glossary** .................................................................................................. 175

**References** ............................................................................................... 181

**Index** ...................................................................................................... 185

# List of Figures

1.1. Inexperienced car mechanic ........................................................................12
1.2. Experienced car mechanic remembering cases............................................12
1.3. Car mechanics learning new cases (cartoons by Yurdagün Göker)............13
1.4. Positioning case-based decision support and alternative techniques ..........16

2.1. User interface for the SIMATIC textual CBR system (see Annex A)........23
2.2. User interface of a conversational CBR system ........................................25
2.3. An object-oriented domain model for sales support of PCs .......................26
2.4. Consultation screen from a structural CBR system ...................................28
2.5. Comparison of efforts for the different CBR approaches...........................33
2.6. The CBR cycle according to Aamodt and Plaza (1994) ............................34

3.1. Support layers at the CAD/CAM help-desk ...............................................36
3.2. Software tools used by the help-desk operators.........................................37
3.3. Knowledge acquisition and transfer ...........................................................38
3.4. Basic structure of a help-desk case.............................................................39
3.5. Domain modeling .........................................................................................41
3.6. The help-desk tool ........................................................................................42
3.7. System architecture......................................................................................43
3.8. "Less is better" similarity graph .................................................................50
3.9. Query screen for Op Amps product search (DYNAMIC) ..........................51
3.10. Query screen for Op Amps product search (OTHER)................................51
3.11. Results display (DYNAMIC) ......................................................................52
3.12. Results display (OTHER)............................................................................53
3.13. Results held from an individual search.......................................................54
3.14. Subpart of the model hierarchy for a complex equipment "Chain of
      Traction"......................................................................................................56
3.15. Submodel CHQQT43 ...................................................................................57
3.16. Data transferred from the TGV for on-board network analysis..................59
3.17. Communication between the diagnostic tool and the databases ..................60

5.1. The experience factory approach (adapted from Basili et al., 1994) ..........81
5.2. The quality improvement paradigm (QIP)...................................................82
5.3. Basic elements of a process model ..............................................................83

5.4.    Structure of the experience base ................................................................85
5.5.    How to use the experience base ...............................................................87
5.6.    Adding new experience ...........................................................................89

6.1.    Interaction among processes.....................................................................94
6.2.    Two alternative complex methods.............................................................94
6.3.    Product flow for the complex method "Prototype Building" ....................95
6.4.    Road map of description sheets ................................................................97
6.5.    Example process description sheet ...........................................................99
6.6.    Example product description sheet..........................................................101
6.7.    Example simple method description sheet................................................102
6.8.    Example complex method description sheet.............................................103

7.1.    Basic structure of a help-desk case .........................................................119
7.2.    Utilization of the case-based help-desk support system ...........................121
7.3.    Project planning and initialization ..........................................................124
7.4.    Implementation of a rapid prototype .......................................................125
7.5.    Evaluation and revision of the prototype.................................................125
7.6.    Implementation of the integrated case-based help-desk support system ...126
7.7.    Evaluation and revision of the case-based help-desk support system........127
7.8.    Utilization of the Case-Based Help-Desk Support System......................128

8.1.    Creating a specialized type .....................................................................137
8.2.    IRSA search results dialog on the Web ...................................................138
8.3.    Process model for catalog search application ...........................................139
8.4.    Process decomposition for requirements acquisition................................140
8.5.    Case base development process decomposition .......................................142
8.6.    Graphical user interface development process .........................................143
8.7.    Implement CBR search engine process ...................................................144
8.8.    Integrate CBR and GUI process .............................................................145

9.1.    The decomposition of a complex piece of equipment ..............................150
9.2.    Process model for building the hierarchical models................................152
9.3.    Process model for case acquisition ..........................................................154

# List of Tables

2.1a. Comparison of the different CBR approaches..............................................29
2.1b. Comparison of the different CBR approaches..............................................30
2.2. Comparison of the efforts required for the different approaches.................32

7.1. Processes during case-based help-desk support system development
and use................................................................................................................111
7.2. Sample form for initial case acquisition ....................................................118

# List of Contributors

**Eric Auriol**
AcknoSoft
15 rue Soufflot
75005 Paris – France

auriol@acknosoft.fr
www.acknosoft.com

**Ralph Bergmann**
University of Kaiserslautern
Department of Computer Science
P.O. Box 3049
67653 Kaiserslautern - Germany

bergmann@informatik.uni-kl.de
wwwagr.informatik.uni-kl.de/~bergmann

**Sean Breen**
IMS
Clara House
Glenegeary Park
Co. Dublin – Ireland

sbreen@imsgrp.com
www.imsgrp.com /imm

**Mehmet Göker**
DaimlerChrysler AG
Forschung und Technologie 3
P.O. Box 2360
89013 Ulm – Germany

mehmet.goeker@daimlerchrysler.com
www.daimlerchrysler.com

**Roy Johnston**
IMS
Clara House
Glenegeary Park
Co. Dublin – Ireland

rjohnston@imsgrp.com
www.imsgrp.com /imm

**Michel Manago**
AcknoSoft
15 rue Soufflot
75005 Paris - France

manago@acknosoft.fr
www.acknosoft.fr

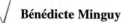

**Bénédicte Minguy**
AcknoSoft
15 rue Soufflot
75005 Paris - France

minguy@acknosoft.fr
www.acknosoft.fr

**Ralph Traphöner**
TECINNO GmbH
Sauerwiesen 2
67661 Kaiserslautern – Germany

traphoener@tecinno.com
www.tecinno.com

**Sascha Schmitt**
University of Kaiserslautern
Department of Computer Science
P.O. Box 3049
67653 Kaiserslautern - Germany

sschmitt@informatik.uni-kl.de
wwwagr.informatik.uni-kl.de/~sschmitt

**Stefan Wess**
TECINNO GmbH
Sauerwiesen 2
67661 Kaiserslautern – Germany

wess@tecinno.com
www.tecinno.com

# About this Book

## Scope of the Book

With this book you can learn a proven method for solving business problems. And you'll come to understand why this methodology is the right solution for you. It addresses issues that are important for both software managers and technical staff. The issues discussed will be particularly useful before the start or the set-up of an investment in building a case-based application. This book aims at increasing:

— case-based decision support software quality
— case data quality
— process productivity for developing case-based applications.

It incorporates the results of seven years of joint international research and development made by the leading specialists from industry and academia.

## Who Should Read This Book

The book is targeted to everyone who has an interest in practical issues about developing case-based applications, in particular integrators, and to everyone who wants to increase her/his understanding of the process and requirements for building such solutions. In particular, this book is addressed to:

— consultants or integrators who want to develop case-based applications,
— end-users or prospective end -users of case-based technologies,
— IT managers,
— QA personnel,
— MIS or software engineering executives.

## The INRECA Consortium

The methodology described in these pages was developed by INRECA, a European consortium created in 1992 by three companies and a university:

- **AcknoSoft**, a French company specializing in data mining,
- **TECINNO**, a German company specializing in Case-Based Reasoning,
- **IMS**, an Irish company that is a software integrator,
- **University of Kaiserslautern in Germany**, where a group headed by Prof. Dr. Michael M. Richter forms a renowned international research center with expertise in CBR.

The INRECA consortium received support from the European Commission through the ESPRIT program. The consortium's goal was to develop innovative technologies to help people make smarter business decisions more quickly by using *cases*, and to integrate these technologies into a single software platform that would allow the technologies to be used more widely. By *case*, we mean a record of a particular past experience that can be reused in the future. For example, in a technical support application, a case is the description of a problem and of its solution. In a sales support application, a case is the description of the characteristics of a product and a reference to that product.

These goals were achieved in late 1995: the consortium was successful both in developing and integrating technologies, and in demonstrating their usefulness for a large-scale industrial application (diagnostic of Boeing 737 engines).

In 1996, the INRECA consortium was expanded to include the multi-national company **DaimlerChrysler**, a large user of INRECA's technology. The emphasis shifted from technology to methodology, because case-based decision-support systems require quality cases that must be maintained over time.

## Why a Methodology?

Case-based solutions are not ready-made solutions. A development process is necessary in order to acquire an appropriate set of cases and to customize the system. The later includes customizing the user interface, as well as the way the system retrieves and processes cases afterwards. The resulting cases may be shown to the user in different ways, and/or the retrieved cases may be adapted. For example, in a cost-estimation application, a quotation that was made three years ago must be adapted, i.e., updated to take inflation into account.

The developers of case-based solutions must master the development process. If the cases are of low quality, because they are poorly represented inside the computer, because they contain errors, or because information is missing, then the quality of the decisions proposed also will be low.

When the INRECA consortium started to address methodological issues, building a case-based solution was mostly an art mastered by only a few. Now that the INRECA methodology is available, building a case-based solution is an industrial process that enables

1. developing case-based applications in a consistent manner,
2. building an experience repository about how to develop case-based applications in order to more quickly reuse this experience for similar projects and to more accurately estimate the efforts that will be required,
3. documenting the development in a standardized way and producing results that are in line with existing quality standards, such as ISO 9000 or SPICE.

## The INRECA Center for Case-Based Solutions

The methodology developed by INRECA needs to live on. Although INRECA's founders will keep contributing their experiences to help the methodology progress and the market grow, it is now time for the methodology to live its own life in a vendor-independent way in order to gain wider recognition. The consortium has, thus, decided to make it publicly available and to financially support the creation of the INRECA center for case-based application. The role of this international center is to promote, maintain, and enhance the methodology. Operated by the University of Kaiserslautern, the center welcomes your comments about the methodology, as well as your contributions to its further development. Please consult the Web site **www.inreca.org** on a regular basis for further information about the center.

## Contents of the Book

This book contains three parts: Part I "Smarter Business with Case-Based Decision Support," Part II "Developing Case-Based Application with the INRECA Methodology," Part III "Using the Methodology in Different Domains."

**Part I: Smarter Business with Case-Based Decision Support.** This first part of the book *(chapters 1 through 3)* shows how captured experience stored as a set of cases improves business in different areas such as help-desk applications, technical diagnosis and maintenance, and intelligent sales support. Chapter 1 gives a brief introduction to Case-Based Reasoning (CBR) and positions it with respect to related technologies, such as databases, statistics, and expert systems. Chapter 2 introduces and compares three different CBR approaches that are implemented in current commercial CBR software: the textual CBR approach, the conversational CBR approach, and the structural CBR approach. Chapter 3 describes three applications of the structural CBR approach developed using the INRECA methodology: The case-based help-desk support system HOMER, the Analog Devices sales support application for operational amplifiers, and the case-based maintenance application for the high-speed train TGV.

**Part II: Developing Case-Based Application with the INRECA Methodology.** The second part of the book *(chapters 4 through 6)* explains in detail the core of the INRECA methodology. We explain how CBR development experience is captured, documented, and reused to enable effective and successful CBR projects. Chapter 4 presents practical guidelines for CBR application development, introducing the general steps that occur in almost every CBR project. Then, chapter 5 introduces the foundations of the INRECA methodology, which are essential for professional CBR application development. Chapters 6 describes in detail how to use software process models to structure and document CBR development projects and how to use the INRECA methodology tool to publish this experience on an Intranet or the Internet to enable efficient project planning.

**Part III: Using the Methodology in Different Domains.** Part III *(chapters 7 through 9)* presents, for three major application areas, how to develop CBR applications according to the INRECA methodology. Building on the foundations laid in part II of the book, lessons learned and reusable software process models are presented in detail. Chapter 7 addresses the application area of case-based help-desk support systems for complex equipment. Chapter 8 deals with developing intelligent catalog search applications. Chapter 9 shows how to develop maintenance applications for technical equipment. Further, for these three application areas, the impact of applying the INRECA methodology is evaluated. Finally, Annex A presents a compilation of success stories of CBR applications developed according to the INRECA methodology.

# Acknowledgments

This book would never have been possible to write without the contributions of several persons and organizations. The idea of the book came during the course of the ESPRIT IV project INRECA II (P22196), which is a successor of the ESPRIT III project INRECA I (P6322). We are, therefore, indebted to the Commission of European Communities Directorate General XIII and in particular to our projects officers Patrick Corsi and Brice Lepape. We would also like to thank the reviewers of the INRECA projects who have always pushed us in positive ways for improved results: Agnar Aamodt (University of Trondheim, Norway), Patricia Arundel (PMA Associates), Rick Magaldi (British Airways, England), Robin Muire (Rolls Royce Plc, England), and last but not least Gerhard Strube (University of Freiburg, Germany).

Because of the number of people involved in the writing of this book, it was unfortunately not possible to mention all the authors on the front cover, and we decided to include only one main author per organization involved in INRECA. The following is a list of additional authors for the current book: Eric Auriol, Roy Johnston, Bénédicte Minguy, Sascha Schmitt, and Ralph Traphöner.

The following persons have helped by contributing background material for the book: Klaus-Dieter Althoff, Brigitte Bartsch-Spörl, Gaddo Benedetti, Martin Bräuer, Michael Carmody, Laurent Champion, Steven Clinton, Christophe Deniard, Stefan Dittrich, Derek Ennis, Nicola Faull, Sylvie Garry, Arlette Gaulène, Yurdagün Göker, Elena Levandowky, Gholamreza Nakhaeizadeh, Póol Macanultaigh, Thomas Pantleon, Carsten Priebisch, Michael M. Richter, Thomas Roth-Berghofer, Arnaud Schleich, Jürgen Schumacher, Reinhard Skuppin, Armin Stahl, Jutta Stehr, Markus Stopmann, Emmanuelle Tartarin-Fayol, and Wolfgang Wilke. For their important contributions, we offer our deepest thanks.

We also thank Susan Branting for the great job she did on proofreading and editing the manuscript of this book within an extremely short period of time. She significantly helped to improve the readability, language, and spelling of the whole text.

# Part I

# Smarter Business with Case-Based Decision Support

This first part of the book, which consists of the chapter 1 through 3, shows how captured experience stored as a set of cases enables smarter business in different areas such as help-desk support, technical diagnosis and maintenance, and intelligent sales support.

**Chapter 1** "Making Smarter Business Decisions in Less Time" gives a brief introduction to Case-Based Reasoning and positions it with respect to related technologies, such as databases, statistics, and expert systems.

**Chapter 2** "Case-Based Reasoning Approaches" introduces and compares three different CBR approaches that are implemented in current commercial CBR software: the textual CBR approach, the conversational CBR approach, and the structural CBR approach approach.

**Chapter 3** "Selected Applications of the Structural Case-Based Reasoning Approach" describes three applications developed using the INRECA methodology: The case-based help-desk support system HOMER, the Analog Devices sales support application for operational amplifiers, and the case-based maintenance application for the high-speed train TGV.

# 1. Making Smarter Business Decisions in Less Time

A case-based information system helps to exploit data so that smarter business decisions can be made in less time and/or at lower cost. This is particularly important for customer relationship management (CRM). Customers need knowledge about products and often require help finding the best products to fit their needs. Once they have purchased a product, they often need technical support. Case-based decision support is uniquely able to help companies learn from experience, manage their corporate knowledge as a valuable asset, and support customers both in pre- and after-sales activities. Case-based decision support encompass both Case-Based Reasoning (CBR) technology, which retrieves cases that are similar to a query, and data mining in order to analyze past queries in order to extract general patterns and rules. Consequently, case-based decision support plays a role for both operational CRM (front office) to help fulfill a short term customer request as well as for analytical CRM to extract knowledge about customers, enhancing a company's understanding of their needs, behavior and long term expectations. This is increasingly important to corporations as they seek to establish long-term relationships with their customers.

## 1.1  Why Case-Based Decision Support?

Thanks to modern electronic systems, the amount of information available in various forms has grown exponentially. On a $1,000 laptop computer, you can subscribe to information sources across multiple corporate data stores: electronic documents, faxes, emails, databases, datawarehouses, CD-ROMs and Web servers. Not only might you feel overwhelmed, but being able to access the right piece of information at the right time is a major issue. We often hear users complain that their corporate databases work predominantly in write-only mode. Yet, this mass of data could reveal strategic knowledge: the marketing department wants to discover trends in buyer behavior, the customer support division must work more efficiently so that the company retains its customers, the financial department wants to more accurately assess risks, and the company as a whole must improve quality management and control. Going from data to decisions is not easy, however.

A case-based information system helps exploit data so that smarter business decisions can be made in less time and/or at lower cost. This is particularly important for customer relation management (CRM). Case-based solutions increasingly play a key role in customer service, sales automation, and even marketing automation (that is, in the front office). We also believe that case-based decision support can play a major role in analytical CRM, bringing value-added business domain knowledge on top of customer data marts. This is increasingly important to corporations as they seek to establish long-term relationships with customers.

According to the Meta Group, "Companies have an opportunity to create a new class of applications based on collaboration components such as human expertise tracking, competitive intelligence, and product innovation. Collaboration will also be a major element in customer relationship management initiatives." We believe that case-based decision support is strategic to achieving collaboration so that

- case knowledge can be preserved, even after the decision maker has left the company,
- employees of the company can share their experience as documented cases, and
- case knowledge can be transferred from skilled experts to novices.

Case-based decision support is a broad area encompassing the front office flow and anything that exists to improve the relationship with both the customer and customer service. A case-based information system is best viewed as a set of processes that continually listens to and extracts knowledge about customers, enhancing a company's understanding of their needs, expectations, and behavior, and thus enabling it to dynamically respond to opportunities. The scope is vast because customer support covers both internal and external customers, as well as marketing, sales, post-sales, and, ultimately, quality-management functions.

Case-based decision support has come along at just the right time. Customers need knowledge about products and often require help finding the best products to fit their needs. And once they have purchased a product, they need support. Case-based decision support is uniquely able to help companies learn from experience, manage their corporate knowledge as a valuable asset, and support customers both in pre- and post-sales activities. Early adopters of case-based decision support solutions, such as Analog devices, Legrand, and Siemens, have empowered their customers to make better informed product choices while providing them with efficient technical support tailored to their needs.

## 1.2  What Is Case-Based Decision Support?

Case-based decision support is both a methodology that models human reasoning and thinking and a methodology for building intelligent computer systems. Cases are stored in memory, and the case-based decision support system analyzes them to retrieve similar cases from memory for decision making. This is the principle underlying Case-Based Reasoning (CBR) technologies.

Case-based decision support can also analyze cases so as to extract patterns and discover knowledge hidden in data. This is the principle underlying *data mining technologies* such as induction.

### 1.2.1  Case-Based Reasoning

Consider a simple example of CBR[1] that deals with car diagnostic. A case stored in the case base is a fault that has been solved in the past. The case description is made of client effects, such as observed symptoms (e.g., engine does not start) and context parameters (e.g., ignition key is turned on). It can also include measured parameters (e.g., state of the electronic control units as obtained using some testing equipment). The solution is the maintenance operation. With CBR, you can make use of the experience captured in this case base to solve new diagnostic problems. If you encounter a new, unsolved diagnostic problem, a past case that is similar to your new problem will very likely contain an appropriate maintenance operation.

---

[1] For technical and research oriented background information about CBR consult one of the following books: Leake (1996), Lenz et al. (1998), Stolpman & Wess (1999), or the CBR-Web at the University of Kaiserslautern at www.cbr-web.org.

**Fig. 1.1.** Inexperienced car mechanic.

How does this process relate to human reasoning? When confronted with a new problem, a technician with no or little experience may attempt to analyze the problem using a Fault Isolation Manual, if there is one and if this is not an overly time-consuming task. He might also try to find the source of the problem by himself, in which case he may end up changing the wrong parts. Finally, he might try ask for help, either by calling the car manufacturer's technical support center or by asking a more experienced colleague.

**Fig. 1.2.** Experienced car mechanic remembering cases.

A more-experienced mechanic can recall past cases he has solved. His intuitive thinking process is, "Have I ever seen a similar problem before? If so, what did I do to solve it?" If the more-experienced mechanic can find the solution and fix the car, his less-experienced colleague will learn from this new experience and build up his own memory of solved cases. This human ability to learn is a key to human intelligence and reasoning.

If the experiences of its employees is indeed a valuable asset to a company, it makes sense to try to capture this experience and store it in a such a way that it can be reused in the future and shared among the company's individuals.

**Fig. 1.3.** Car mechanics learning new cases (cartoons by Yurdagün Göker).

The principles of CBR are the same. Cases are captured and stored in a way that they can be reused. CBR retrieves the appropriate cases when they are needed. These are presented to the user so that he can decide whether the solution that worked in the past will solve the new problem.

### 1.2.2. Knowledge Discovery and Data Mining

Consider a simple example of knowledge discovery. Once a person has accumulated a large number of similar cases, he starts making generalizations. When he sees a new instance of the same case, he no longer needs to recall previous ones. He just knows that for a certain pattern of faults, this is the solution that will work. For example, when he turns on the ignition key and there is no light on the control panel, he knows that it is because there is no power and that the battery is probably dead. This ability to learn from experience by extracting general laws is also a key to human intelligence. Certain data mining techniques, in particular induction, aim at discovering general knowledge that is hidden in data.

Induction goes from the specific to the general, deduction from the general to the specific. In deduction, there are some general rules, such as "all humans are mortal." From a specific fact, such as "Socrates is a human," the new fact, "Socrates is mortal," is deduced. Induction is the reverse process. If we know that "Socrates is mortal and Socrates is a human," "Stefan is mortal and Stefan is a human," "Ralph is mortal and Ralph is a human," "Elena is mortal and Elena is a human," and so on, the general rule "all humans are mortal" can be induced, and we produce a generalization of the data.

The benefit of having learned such general knowledge after analyzing cases is that the knowledge can be used to solve new problems more quickly. It might also help discover patterns in unwanted events. For instance, we may have an unusually high rate of problems with a certain pattern for a car with air conditioning. This information can be fed back to customer service so that a service bulletin can be issued to warn all mechanics about the problem. It also might be sent to the R&D department so R&D can make a design change to the vehicle that will prevent a reoccurrence of the problem. These patterns might also be used to make predictions and detect problems early (prognostic).

## 1.3  Successful Applications of Case-Based Decision Support

Case-based decision support is being used daily to help make better business decisions in a variety of industries, such as automotive, manufacturing, electronics, computers, telecommunications, petroleum, transportation, banking, insurance, and health care, as well as in biology and environmental protection. The following sections give examples of domains for case-based decision support.

### 1.3.1  Management of Industrial Knowledge

Knowledge about manufacturing processes and quality management is disseminated across various departments and databases: marketing, design, production, after-sales, and so on. A case-based decision support system capitalizes on this know-how and helps preserve manufacturing knowledge, reducing product-development cycles and improving quality.

### 1.3.2  Sales Support

Selling, estimating production costs, making a quotation for products that are made on demand, or doing market analysis are all activities that benefit from case-based decision support. Companies can develop sales catalogs that feature only products that best match customer needs and that are ranked according to how well they match earlier patterns of buying. Such catalogs can be made available over the Internet in intelligent Electronic Commerce Applications.

### 1.3.3  Reliability Analysis

A systematic analysis of past incidents reduces the risk of accidents. By identifying human and equipment risk factors, monitoring machines, and analyzing alarms that censors automatically generate, case-based decision support increases the reliability of mission-critical equipment.

### 1.3.4 Technical Support

From the diagnostic tools of field technicians (mobile office) to the help-desk at the after-sales customer support department (front office), case-based decision support helps solve problems more quickly and accurately. Case-based decision support significantly reduces the cost of finding a solution.

## 1.4 Benefits of Case-Based Decision Support

Benefits of using case-based decision support are:

— finding the solution to complex problems more quickly,
— discovering decision knowledge hidden in data,
— transferring experience from skilled specialists to novices,
— building a corporate memory by sharing individual experiences,

Case-based technologies enable companies to build powerful decision-support solutions. Some examples of benefits from case-based applications are:

— a leading aerospace corporation reduced airplane downtime by 25%,
— a help-desk system for robot maintenance, developed in fewer than six months, significantly improved customer support service and helped cut down costs for training new service technicians,
— a leading manufacturer of electrical supplies can more quickly and accurately estimate the cost of manufacturing plastic parts,
— a small company saved 25% on the cost of repairing electronic boards,
— a leading US manufacturer of electronic devices delivered an intelligent sales support system on 120,000 CD-ROMs and on the Internet to find products that best matched customer demands, increasing sales significantly,
— in just two months, a major company in the business of computer maintenance went from 5% problems solved over the phone without sending a technician to the customer's site to 30% problems solved on first call. This generated paybacks for the project in fewer than 10 weeks.

## 1.5 Case-Based Decision Support and Alternative Techniques

Several technical publications have been published to allow comparison of case-based decision support and alternative techniques, such as classical statistics, expert systems, neural networks, and databases (see, for example, Althoff et al., 1995).

The difference between case-based decision support and these alternative techniques is not only a question of which algorithms are used. Case-based decision support is designed to help people make decisions about individual cases. It does not aim at finding the right solution but at helping people to find the right solution by presenting the appropriate cases when they are needed.

In the following, we briefly position case-based decision support with respect to these alternative techniques (see also Fig. 1.4).

### 1.5.1 Statistics

Techniques such as statistics are primarily used to analyze populations so decisions about individual cases can be made. Should safety and reliability system in a nuclear power plant warn the user that a particular case looks very similar to the pattern of the Chernobyl accident, or should the case be ignore because it is not statistically significant?

### 1.5.2 Expert Systems

Compared to expert systems, case-based decision support systems do not rely on rules that are supplied by a specialist. Specialists work out concrete problems and describe them, using their every day language, in order to set up the domain model, if there is one, and the case base. It is a natural approach: the specialist is never asked to supply diagnostic rules or to define formal specifications of a decision process. The knowledge is easier to acquire and is easier to maintain because the system can learn new cases.

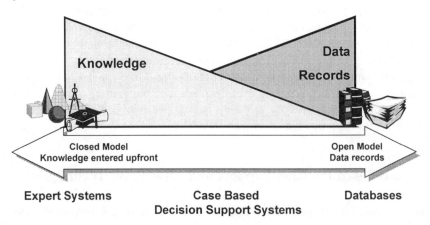

**Fig. 1.4.** Positioning case based decision support and alternative techniques.

### 1.5.3  Databases

Classical database technology offers languages such as SQL, which can retrieve cases that exactly match the query the user enters. On the other hand, case-based decision support can find cases that are similar but not necessarily identical. It performs fuzzy searches (also called *parametric searches*) and automatically finds keys for discriminating among cases. Similarity-based parametric searches are far more flexible than other parametric search techniques, because they do not rely on assumptions, such as "parameters that are entered first are more important."

## 1.6  Development Process and Case Collection

A case-based system is not a ready-made solution; cases are different from application to application: a case that describes an airplane engine fault for a technical support application is described differently than is a case for a product that can be bought in a sales-support application. The general development process is to:

— build and maintain a case base,
— customize the user interface,
— tune the way the information system operates.

For example, the system's developer can indicate how to compute the similarity for a give feature that describes a case, how the case base is organized inside the computer memory, and/or how individual cases are reused and adapted once they have been retrieved.

If the case base evolves over time, as it is usually does, an organization and the appropriate process must be put in place. An existing organization may also be adapted to support case collection and quality control. For example, in the aerospace industry, manufacturers often have technical representatives in the airlines who can collect and validate the technical content of the data that is fed back to the case base. A case-based application is only as good as the case base on which it operates.

The effort required to build an application varies drastically. In a technical diagnostic application, building up a well-populated, high-quality case base can take six months and consume 80% of the efforts; while customizing the user interface and the retrieval uses only 20%. This ratio might be completely reversed for a sales-support application where the data is an existing catalog of products. The catalog only requires some reformatting, but the bulk of the effort goes into customizing the user interface and the way the retrieval engine operates. This is one reason editors of case-based tools have produced *vertical platforms* for specific domains, for instance, different vertical platforms for help-desk applications and sales-support applications.

To help you understand the concept of a vertical platform, we'll use an analogy. Software used to build accounting software is not a specific application. For instance, the accounting module of an Enterprise Resource Planning (ERP) system, such as SAP or Baan, can be used to build different accounting applications. Each application may require some specific customization, and the customization effort may sometime be quite significant. A company that has stocks will require a different interface and implement different accounting rules than will a pure consulting firm that does not have stocks. Customizations can even include national parameters: a French company will use different accounting rules than a British one, yet the same accounting module can be used with some level of customization to develop both. The accounting software relies on a standard generic database management system (DBMS), such as Oracle or Sybase, but it is simpler for a software integrator to use the vertical platform to develop a specific accounting application than it is to develop it from scratch using Oracle or Sybase.

The concept of a vertical platform for developing case-based decision support applications is the same. A vertical platform is dedicated to specific tasks, such as building a help-desk. It is often implemented using a general purpose case-based decision support engine but incorporates application-specific modifications and add-ons, such as in the following instances:

1.  There is a default, pre-defined business process and a proposed development methodology. For example, there is a default process to acquire and control the quality of a case base in a help-desk environment on a local network. Cases are put on a server with different statuses (current case, closed case that has not yet been reviewed, reference case reviewed by a steering committee).
2.  There may be additional specific modules that are tailor-made for the market that is being addressed. For example, a call-tracking module is usually offered for help-desk applications.
3.  It is easier to market and to license the software to users and integrators (e.g., value added resellers) who not only don't understand the core technology but don't care.

## 1.7  How Are Cases Retrieved?

A CBR system needs some mechanism for retrieving similar cases from the case base. There are different approaches, depending on the case representation that was chosen. Text-based CBR systems use a keyword-driven approach. Conversational CBR systems usually have a hard-coded selection approach. CBR systems that follow the structured data approach sometimes offer the possibility of customizing the way the similarity is computed. The underlying technique used is called *nearest neighbor retrieval*. The global similarity between cases can be computed, for example, as the weighted sum of a local similarity that is computed for each feature used to describe a case. Different metrics are employed for computing the local similarity for each individual feature according to its data type (numbers, symbols, and so on). Each feature may have a weight associated with it to increase or decrease its overall importance. In some systems, the way the local similarity is computed can be customized for a specific feature. This is achieved by programming a function that returns the similarity between the two cases for the specific feature or by using a pre-defined similarity editor.

If the case base is reasonably large, it must be indexed. Different indexing mechanisms are available. Trees can be used to index large case bases. A decision tree is a hierarchical partitioning of the stored cases, based on the feature values. Its root node contains all the cases, while lower nodes progressively partition cases into subsets according to the various features applied in order of discriminatory power. The decision tree determines the order in which tests should be applied during consultation so cases can be retrieved. In some case-based decision support systems, decision trees are produced automatically by analyzing the cases using induction, based on data mining techniques. Induction can discover the most discriminatory features and use these to produce trees that are well balanced and not very deep so that cases can be efficiently retrieved by checking the value of a minimal number of features.

Static decision trees generated by induction may perform badly if the value of a particular feature is not known during case retrieval (i.e., during the consultation by the case-based decision support system). An alternative is to generate the decision tree on the fly and, if the value of a given feature cannot be known, use the next best one and so on. In case of an interactive consultation system where a question is associated with the feature (e.g., what is the state of the lights), the order of the questions is not fixed but, rather, context dependent. This technique is known as *dynamic induction*. If the questions are asked one by one, it is called *system guided dynamic induction*. This is well adapted for low-skilled users who want to be guided step by step. Sometimes a list of questions is displayed on the screen, with the "best" (most discriminatory) questions at the top of the list, and the user can select the question(s) he prefers to answer. This is called *user guided dynamic induction*. This kind of induction is appropriate for users who have a high level of expertise and who want to answer directly the questions they believe are relevant.

## 1.8  How Are Cases Represented?

The first step in building a case-based application is to decide how to represent a case inside the computer. This will have an impact on how the case is stored (in a database, in a binary file, in an electronic document, and so on.), how the CBR retrieval engine will perform, and what kind of knowledge can be discovered by the data mining engine. In commercially available systems, there are different approaches to case representation and, related to that, different techniques for Case-Based Reasoning: the *textual CBR approach*, the *conversational CBR approach*, and the *structural CBR approach*.

In the textual CBR approach, cases are represented in free-text form. In the conversational CBR approach, cases are lists of questions and answers. For every case, there can be different questions. In the structural CBR approach, the developer of the case-based solution decides ahead of time what features will be relevant when describing a case and then stores the cases according to these. For a real estate application, these features might include price, number of rooms, number of square feet, location, and so on, and the outcome may be the specific apartment that can be sold or rented. This structured set of features is known as the *domain model*

In chapter 2, we describe these three approaches in more details and compare them.

# 2. Case-Based Reasoning Approaches

Case-Based Reasoning means learning from previous experiences. Given the fact that this is a very general approach to human problem-solving behavior, it is more than natural that there are different approaches for implementing this process on computer systems. In commercial CBR systems, there are three main approaches that differ in the sources, materials, and knowledge they use.

The *textual CBR approach* eases case acquisition. It is very useful in domains where large collections of know-how documents already exist and the intended user is able to immediately make use of the knowledge contained in the respective documents. The approach is well suited when there are not too many cases at a time (less than a couple of hundred) and when each case has a short description (three sentences at most). Otherwise, textual CBR retrieves a large number of cases that are irrelevant. The cost for controlling the quality of textual CBR is high.

The *conversational CBR approach* is very useful for domains where a high volume of simple problems must be solved again and again. The system guides the agent and the customer with predefined dialogs. However, the case base is organized manually by the case author, which is a complex and costly activity when the cases are described by many attributes (questions). The conversational approach is well suited for applications in which only a few questions are needed for decision making. Maintenance costs are high because the developer must manually position each new case in a decision tree-like structure and update the ordering of the questions.

The *structural CBR approach* relies on cases that are described with attributes and values that are pre-defined. In different structural CBR systems, attributes may be organized as flat tables, or as sets of tables with relations, or they may be structured in object-oriented manner. The structural CBR approach is useful in domains where additional knowledge, beside cases, must be used in order to produce good results. The domain model insures that new cases are of high quality and the maintenance effort is low. This approach always gives better results than the two others, but it requires an initial investment to produce the domain model.

## 2.1  The Textual CBR Approach

The developer of the case-based solution may decide to have cases recorded as free text. For example, this may be product descriptions or service reports. The CBR retrieval engine then uses various keyword matching techniques to retrieve cases. This can be based on string searches or on N-grams. N-grams is a technique that consists in separating words into lists of N characters. For example, for tri-grams, the word "akunamatata" is turned into the list of three characters ("aku" "kun" "una" "nam" "ama" "mat" "ata" "tat" "ata"). Both the query and the case base are transformed, and case matching is performed on these. This technique is robust when there are spelling mistakes. A word like "aknamatata" would be recognized as similar to "akunamatata". The main disadvantage of N-grams is that when there are large block of texts with many words, almost anything matches everything.

To assess the quality of a textual CBR system, two parameters are used: *recall* and *precision*. Recall measures how many cases from the set of existing relevant cases are retrieved. Precision measures how many of the retrieved cases are relevant. As the case base grows, there is often high recall but low precision. This means that the system retrieves many cases, but only few of these are relevant.

**Example: Frequently Asked Questions.** A company has a collection of documents that represent the current set of frequently asked questions at the company's hotline. Each document contains a single problem and its solution. Navigating and searching in the list of documents is difficult for customers as well as for the people working on the hotline. To avoid this unfriendly search process, customers tend to call the company's hotline instead of solving the well-known problems on their own. The result is that the traffic at the hotline is constantly increasing. The goal of the CBR system is to help customers and employees find solutions to problems whose solutions are already known and documented.

The following box presents an example of a textual case and Fig. 2.1 shows the user interface of an example textual CBR system. Both are from the SIMATIC Knowledge Manager application, described in Annex A.

---

**Frequently Asked Question 241**

**Title:**     Order numbers of CPUs with which communications is possible.

**Question:**  Which order numbers must the S7-CPUs have to be able to run basic communications with SFCs?

**Answer:**    In order to participate in communications via SFCs without a configured connection table, the module concerned must have the correct order number. The following table illustrates which order number your CPU must have to be able to participate in these S7 homogeneous communications.

---

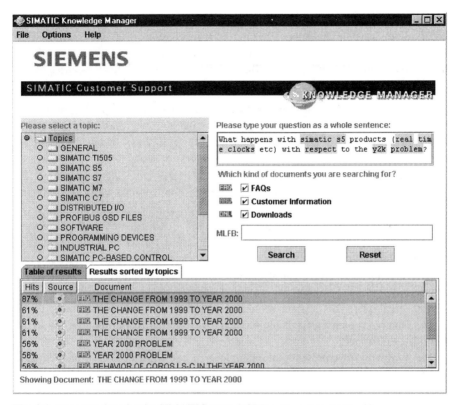

**Fig. 2.1.** User interface for the SIMATIC textual CBR system (see Annex A).

## 2.2  The Conversational CBR Approach

A second approach is called conversational CBR. The principle is to capture the knowledge contained in customer/agent conversations. A case is represented through a list of questions that varies from one case to the other. There is no domain model and no standardized structure for all the cases. This may produce unreliable behavior of the resulting CBR system, which may ask, during consultation, questions that are totally irrelevant (e.g., questions about electrical problems when the user specified the fault is mechanical). To work around this problem, questions to describe the cases are sometime organized into tree-like structures. The developer creates groups of questions that are used to describe a certain subset of the case base. Each case is then positioned by hand in this structure, which must be maintained manually by the developer. This task can be compared to developing an expert system that relies on decision trees.

To index the cases, the case author must also define the order in which the user is asked to answer the questions during the consultation. The work required to develop a conversational approach CBR solution can thus be compared to building an expert system. The difference is that this "expert system" displays cases to the user during the consultation.

**Example: Call Center for Printer Problems.** A company is producing a wide range of different printers for the consumer market. For customer support, it maintains a call center with several agents solving product-related problems by phone. Since the main target market of the company is consumer oriented, most of the problems are simple to solve but the volume of the daily calls is very high. To provide the necessary staff for the call center, the company has hired several part-time agents who should be able to solve most of the simple calls directly. For more advanced problems, the company maintains a highly qualified second-level support team of product specialists. Since the training effort for the first-level agents is constantly increasing and cannot be done just on time anymore, there is a trend that more and more calls are forwarded to the second-level support team. This is not convenient for the customer and causes workload and priority problems at the second level. The CBR system should empower the first-level support agents to solve as many problems as possible on the phone without forwarding the call to the second-level support.

The following box presents an example of a conversational case and Fig. 2.2 shows the user interface of an example conversational CBR system.

---

**Case: 241**
**Title**: Printer does not work in the new release

| | |
|---|---|
| **What kind of problem do you have?** | Printer Problem |
| **Does the printer perform a self-test?** | Yes |
| **Does the printer work with other software?** | Yes |
| **Did you just install the software?** | Yes |
| **Did you create a printer definition file?** | Yes |
| **What release did you install?** | 4.2 |

**Problem:** Installation procedure overrides printer definition
**Action:** Reinstall the printer from disk

---

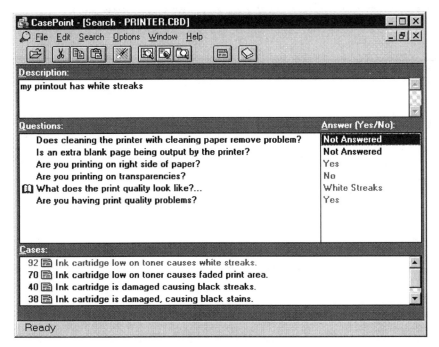

**Fig 2.2.** User interface of a conversational CBR system.


## 2.3  The Structural CBR Approach

The idea underlying the structural CBR approach is to represent cases according to a common structure called the *domain model*. The domain model specifies a set of attributes (also called features) that are used to represent a case. This set of attributes is structured by the domain model. In simple applications, the structure may be a flat table like the one produced by a spreadsheet. In more complex domains, the case description cannot be a flat table. For example, for a robot maintenance application such as Sepro's (see Annex A), electrical problems are described using different attributes than mechanical problems.

A relational or an object data model can be used in such applications. In a relational model, there are several tables that are indexed by a primary key. Each case has a unique key, and the case description is distributed in several tables. The distribution is defined by the relations of the database. In an object-oriented database, objects are decomposed into subobjects. For example, in a PC sales-support application, a PC points to several subobjects, such as screen and hard disk. Each object has its own set of attributes, such as price and the manufacturer (see Fig. 2.3).

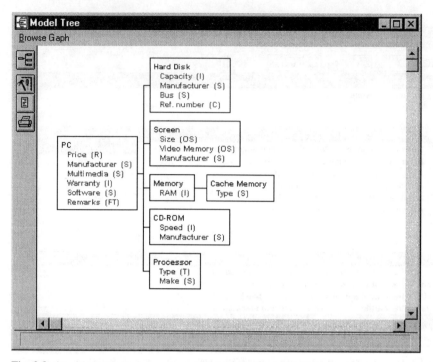

**Fig. 2.3.** An object-oriented domain model for sales support of PCs.

Another important aspect of the structural CBR approach is that each attribute has a specific type. The attribute can be a symbol that takes one or several pre-defined values in a list. For example, the manufacturer of the PC may be Dell, IBM, Hewlett Packard, and so on. The data type can also be a number (integer or real) within a certain range. For example, the price of a PC is a number between $800 and $6,000. Some CBR systems provide additional powerful attribute types. For example, the symbol can be ordered (for example, small, medium, high). A taxonomy type can describe relations of generality among attribute values. For example, for the attribute processor, values P100, P133 are Pentium; P266, P300 are Pentium II, and so on. The ability to represent and use this type of background knowledge can significantly improve the quality of the retrieval for the CBR engine. Background knowledge can be used to discover additional similarities between two cases. For example, if the customer wants to buy a machine with a P366 processor, we would recommend a machine with a P300 (Pentium II) over a machine with a P266 (Pentium).

To summarize, the domain model defines a standard way to represent all cases. Note that this is different from the textual CBR approach, which may contain a structure using languages such as SGML (for example, the question-and-answer headers in the example in the previous chapter), but where the content associated to each header is not standardized (it contains free text). Even if the content of these headers are stored in a database (using what is called *text blobs*), this is not sufficient to qualify for the structural approach. In the structural CBR approach, each attribute must be a field in the database and each value must be standardized.

**Example: Sales Support for Electronic Devices.** A company has described a catalog of electronic products according to the different sales parameters (see the Analog Devices application in section 3.2 and Annex A). Parameters are used to describe technical characteristics of the product, as well as sales characteristics. The application's goal is to find the best matching product based on the characteristics the customer enters for his or her desired product. There are so many characteristics that the chance of retrieving a product that is identical to the user's query is very low (no exact match). Standard database queries almost never retrieve any products from the catalog database.

The following box presents an example of a structural case and Fig. 2.4 shows the user interface of an example conversational CBR system. Both are taken from the Analog Devices application. In the real application, there are about 40 attributes to describe each case. The query is entered by assigning values to the attributes attached to objects input, output, supply, and other characteristics. The result is a list of products that can be compared and are ranked according to their similarity with respect to the query.

| | |
|---|---|
| **Product** | Reference : AD8009<br>Price : 2.25 |
| **Input:** | Input offset voltage : 2 mV<br>Input bias current : 50 uA<br>Open loop gain : 108 dB<br>Input resistance : 110 kohms |
| **Output:** | Output voltage : 1.2 V<br>Output current drive : 175 mA |
| **Supply:** | Single supply : No<br>PSPS : 70 dB |
| **Other:** | Number of devices per package : single<br>Maximum temperature range : IND<br>Available Package(s) : SOIC |

Additional domain knowledge can be entered. For example, information about the fact that for the temperature range a military space certification is more constrained than a SMD certification. When "SMD" is entered for the value of attribute "temperature range" in the query, products having the value "space" for this parameter also match the query.

The structural CBR approach is very useful when quality control of the decision-support system (and the case base) is an important issue. It is also possible to have a multilingual system with a single case base. A dictionary of attributes is

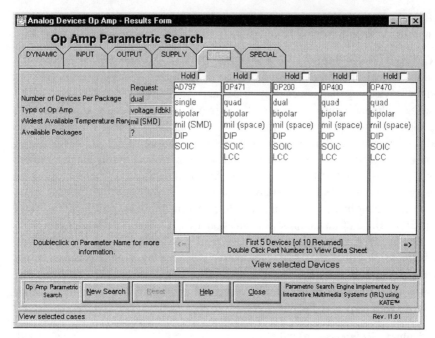

**Fig. 2.4.** Consultation screen from a structural CBR system.

then used to translate the attribute names and the values. Switching to another language amounts to displaying an alternative view of the same case base.

This approach requires an initial investment to come up with the initial domain model. This model usually evolves over the lifecycle of the application: new attributes are added, new values are added. A maintenance process for the domain model is, therefore, required. This is why the INRECA methodology for building and maintaining the domain model and the case base is particularly important.

## 2.4  Comparing the Different Approaches

From a user's point of view, all these approaches look very similar. A query case is entered and similar cases are retrieved from the case base. From a managerial point of view there are important differences that deal with:

1.  the material required to set up the initial case base,
2.  the amount of work needed to maintain the case base,
3.  the effort required to control the accuracy of the CBR system afterward.

Tables 2.1a and 2.1b show a synthetic overall comparison of the different CBR approaches.

**Tab. 2.1a.** Comparison of the different CBR approaches.

| Criteria | Textual CBR | Conversational CBR | Structural CBR |
|---|---|---|---|
| **Case Base** | A case is represented in free-text format. The cases may be structured according to headers, but the content of the headers is in free-text form. The case base is the collection of free texts that may be, for example, in electronic documents that are accessed on the Internet. | Cases are represented by a list of question/answers. The list of questions and answers may vary from one case to another. There is no common data structure. The questions may be stored in a database but each question is not a separate field of the database. | The case base is made out of records in a database. The records contain fields whose values are standardized. Specific cases are recorded by assigning values to the attributes that have been defined. The initial case base may easily be extracted from an existing database. |
| **Query Case** | A query is represented by a question in free-text form whose content is similar to the description part of the stored cases. | A list of questions and answers following a dialog with the user. | The query consists of a set of attribute values. These may be obtained by asking questions. In a technical-support application, attributes are symptoms, operating conditions, and measures. In a sales-support application, attributes are characteristics of the desired products. |
| **Results** | A list of documents that might be useful. | A list of possible actions attached to the cases that have been retrieved. | A list of database records that describe cases. |
| **Background Knowledge** | Dictionaries of similar terms like "install : setup" or "printer : plotter" and information about the relationships between different words. | Ordering of questions, hierarchy of questions in a tree-like structure, possible answers for the questions that have been defined. | Domain model that defines the case structure. Rules to deduce values. Information on how to compute the similarity among attributes values. |

**Tab. 2.1b.** Comparison of the different CBR approaches.

| Criteria | Textual CBR | Conversational CBR | Structural CBR |
|---|---|---|---|
| **Initial Effort** | Defining terms, synonyms and stop-words. Analyzing and setting up relationships between different words. | Storing dialogs within a case base, structuring the questions to organize the case base manually, ordering the questions manually. This can be done by entering existing decision trees. | Defining the domain model. Importing the database or collecting cases according to the structure of the domain model. This can be done, for example, using an electronic questionnaire. |
| **Case Creation** | Writing new documents | Adding new dialogs. Depending on the structure of the dialog, new questions must be entered. | Adding a new record to the database. A questionnaire (forms) can be used in order to use the same vocabulary. |
| **Maintenance** | Maintaining the dictionary of controlled terms and sentences. Analyzing user queries and results. | Maintaining the list of questions and answers. Eliminating doubles, combining answers and questions. Reordering the questions by hand for the consultation. | Maintaining the case base and the domain model. The CBR system must keep up with these modifications. It can automatically compute the order of the questions during consultation |
| **Multilingual Case Bases** | Almost impossible. Must have different case bases. | Difficult, no standard-ized thesaurus of terms. | Easy to implement with a single case base. |
| **Advantages** | Existing documents can be used as cases. No initial investment is required for modeling the cases. | The approach is intuitive and easy to understand. The system asks questions which are answered by the user and this dialog is stored in the case base. | An existing database can be used to produce the initial case base. Creating additional cases can be done without any knowledge about how the CBR system will use the cases afterward. |
| **Drawbacks** | The user is not guided. The CBR system must cope with spelling mistakes. The quality of retrieval depends on the syntax and not on the real content of the cases. High costs for quality control of the CBR system. | No explicit knowledge represented in the system for computing similarity. The interdependencies among different dialogs cannot be predicted. High maintenance costs. | It may be difficult to create a predefined case structure. This can usually be achieved within most technical domains but becomes harder in softer domains. High investment costs. |

If the material already available in the company corresponds to the material expected by the intended user of the system, choosing the CBR approach is natural and easy. The effort needed to set up a CBR system is always minimized in this case, and if the maintenance process for this material is already in place, the CBR system will often directly fit into it.

Unfortunately this is rarely the case. The material available is rarely the kind of material that is really needed for the case base. For example, in a maintenance management system, historical data about machine faults is usually available, but, unfortunately, it rarely contains the technical information that is needed for decision making. When it does, the information is usually very difficult to use. For example, it is not unusual in legacy maintenance management systems to see case descriptions such as the following.

---

**Problem:** Machine was not working and customer was very unhappy.
**Action:** Decided to use a workaround procedure to fix the problem.

---

Such material cannot be used to build a CBR system, because the technical information that is needed does not appear in the case description. Reusing free text fields of a database to initialize a case base is often difficult because the data was collected without guidelines and each case author had complete freedom about how he recorded the information.

## 2.5  Effort Required for the Different Approaches

Table 2.2 summarizes the effort for the different CBR approaches. Each numbers in parentheses refers to an explanatory remark given in the following section. Effort to *reuse existing material* indicates the amount of work that typically is necessary to initially create the case base out of existing material and data. Effort for *initial modeling* refers to the work required to define dictionaries of terms (textual CBR), the initial domain model (structural CBR), or the lists of questions (conversational CBR). With *case creation*, we state the effort required to enter new cases into an existing case base. Effort to *tune the CBR* refers to how the developer or the integrator controls how the CBR engine retrieves cases. This can be, for instance, achieved by tuning the similarity measures, by defining similarities among attributes values, or by setting weights attached to attributes. For example, in a maintenance application, it is preferable to perform two tests that are quick and easy, such as looking at a fault code on a control panel or checking whether a lamp is on, over one that is time consuming and requires, for example, dismantling part of the equipment. With *quality control*, we look at the effort for verifying that the decision support system works correctly and displays accurate results. *Maintenance* refers to the work required for updating the case base and the CBR system when new cases are added.

**Tab. 2.2.** Comparison of the efforts required for the different approaches.

| Effort per Task | Textual | Conversational | Structural |
|---|---|---|---|
| Reuse existing material | Very Low | High (1) | Medium |
| Initial Modeling | High (2) | Low | High (3) |
| Case Creation | Low | High (1) | Medium |
| Tuning CBR | Very high (4) | High/Impossible (5) | Medium-Low |
| Quality Control | Very high (4) | High (6) | Low |
| Maintenance | Low for the case base, High to tune the retrieval (4) | High (6) | Very Low |

(1)   Cases cannot be loaded directly from a database. For each case, the questions are positioned by the developer manually in a tree-like structure. The ordering of the questions is not done automatically like in the structural approach.

(2)   This corresponds to defining the terms, synonyms, stop words.

(3)   This corresponds to defining the database structure, the attributes, and their type (domain model).

(4)   Retrieval is performed using keyword searches or other techniques such as "N-grams." The ability to retrieve a document depends on the syntax of the information reported in the document, not on its true meaning. It is difficult to tune the system so that the right documents are retrieved, and it is also very difficult to maintain this afterward. New documents can drastically alter the retrieval quality (that is, recall and precision).

(5)   This technology does not allow the developer to define similarity, and the system functions as a black box. Developer sometimes defines fake attributes/questions in the case in order to work around the problem.

(6)   The behavior of the retrieval process can be altered when new cases are entered and new questions are defined to describe cases. The ordering of questions is done by the developer, unlike in the structural approach where this is done automatically.

In Fig. 2.5, we compare the effort require to build the initial system and the effort required to maintain it. We see that a structural CBR system requires more effort to create the domain model, but less maintenance effort. The conversational approach requires less work initially but the most work for maintenance. The textual approach is half way between the other two.

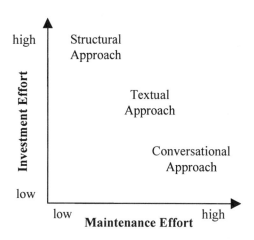

**Fig. 2.5.** Comparison of efforts for the different CBR approaches.

## 2.6  Overall Assessment of the Different CBR Approaches

The basic idea behind all approaches is to retrieve problem-solving experience that has been stored as a case in a case base, adapt and reuse it to solve new problems and, if not successful, learn from failures.

On the abstract level, the CBR process can be described as four main steps (Fig. 2.6): *retrieve, reuse, revise,* and *retain.* While the names for these tasks may vary from one process model to the other, the basic ideas stay the same.

During retrieval the most similar case or cases in the case base are determined, based on the new problem description. During reuse the information and knowledge in the retrieved case(s) is used to solve the new problem. The new problem description is combined with the information contained in the old case to form a solved case. During revision the applicability of the proposed solution is evaluated in the real-world. If necessary and possible, the proposed case must be adapted in some way. If the case solution generated during the revise phase must be kept for future problem solving, the case base is updated with a new learned case in the *retain* phase.

Putting knowledge to work by using CBR is not something that can be done immediately. A process has to be put into place to capture business parameters that are used for decision making, to acquire quality cases that are described according to these parameters, and to maintain the quality of the case base over time. Sometimes, this is not an easy process. One reason for having the INRECA methodology and this book is to make this process clear and understandable, and to

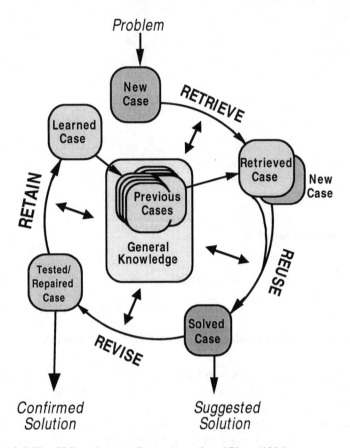

**Fig. 2.6.** The CBR cycle according to Aamodt and Plaza (1994).

document it in a standardized way in order to make it consistent and reproducible. The following chapters describe the INRECA methodology and its applications in detail.

# 3. Selected Applications of the
# Structural Case-Based Reasoning Approach

In this chapter we describe three applications that have been developed using the structural CBR approach and the INRECA methodology: The case-based help-desk support system HOMER, the Analog Devices product catalog, and the case-based maintenance application for the high-speed train TGV. The three systems represent common application areas for CBR techniques. They are distinct in terms of their complexity, the representation and similarity measures that are needed to develop the system, and the processes that have to be put in place to operate the application. Hence, they illustrate the versatility of the INRECA approach and the bandwidth of solutions that can be developed with it.

# 3.1 HOMER: A Case-Based CAD/CAM Help-Desk Support Tool

### 3.1.1 DaimlerChrysler's Motivation

The CAD/CAM help-desk at DaimlerChrysler in Sindelfingen, Germany, provides support for the engineers developing Mercedes-Benz cars. Approximately 1,500 engineers work on workstations, using, on average, 30 different applications.

The amount of hardware and software will increase drastically during the next years. Also, each year one third of all hardware is replaced with new models and each program has about one major and up to four minor updates. Since the number of help-desk personnel will remain constant and the help-desk operation is a central and time-critical operation, some kind of computer support that goes beyond the classical trouble-ticketing systems was needed.

### 3.1.2 Initial Situation at the CAD/CAM Help-Desk

The help-desk in Sindelfingen is organized into three layers (Fig. 3.1). The end-users are engineers developing Mercedes-Benz cars. When the engineers have problems with their software or hardware, the first person they contact is usually the "key-user." This is an engineer working in the same group who has more experience with the software and/or hardware. If the key-user cannot help, the first-level support is contacted. This level is divided into several groups. The system help-desk gives support on the operating system and on simple hardware problems. The application help-desks specialize in certain software programs and provide support in their use and function. If the first-level help-desk cannot solve the problem, the problem goes to the second level, i.e., the system administrators and

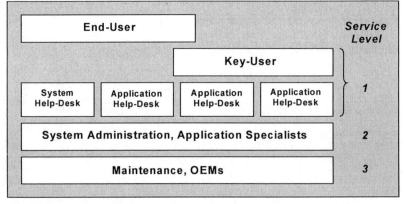

**Fig. 3.1.** Support layers at the CAD/CAM help-desk.

application specialists. Personnel at this level comprises highly skilled and specialized system administrators. Problems are transferred to specific system administrators based on their areas of expertise. Because the overlap in the areas of expertise among the administrators is small, problems have to wait if the required administrator is not available. Problems that cannot be solved by second-level support are transferred to the hardware and software vendors, some of which have in-house representatives.

Initially, the operators at the help-desk were using several software tools to support them during help-desk operations (Fig. 3.2). HIT is a "Help-desk Information Tool" that was developed in-house to give the help-desk operators information about the user and his default environment from the network (NIS). CIVIS is an inventory system that provides maintenance and hardware configuration information to the help-desk operator. FES is a trouble-ticket tool that is used to record, track, and escalate calls.

Even though these tools aid the help-desk operators in performing their tasks, they do not give support in diagnosing problems and cannot serve as a knowledge repository. The growing amount of hard- and software, as well as the goal to drastically shorten development cycles, greatly increases the responsibility of and the pressure on the help-desk.

Although the personnel at the help-desk are well trained, they cannot be knowledgeable in all areas. The complexity and the dynamics of the domain make it infeasible for one help-desk operator to understand and manage all the hardware and software, as well as the network. The end-users, i.e., the engineers, get frustrated when they have to be transferred from one help-desk operator to another, and the operators' self-esteem suffers as well.

Since most problems recur, the operators end up rederiving solutions to problems that a colleague has already solved. This not only frustrates the help-desk operator and the engineer, but also wastes company resources.

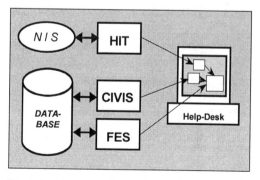

**Fig. 3.2.** Software tools used by the help-desk operators.

### 3.1.3 Project Goals and Benefits

To increase the efficiency and effectiveness of the help-desk, and thereby increase the productivity of car development, it is in the interest of DaimlerChrysler to accumulate the experiences of the help-desk operators in a knowledge repository and make them available to all operators on all levels (Fig. 3.3). This way, corporate knowledge, one of the company's most valuable assets, is preserved and extended, ensuring that solutions to previous problems are available to all levels of the help-desk, whenever and wherever they are needed. The training of new help-desk operators is also expedited. With the accumulated knowledge of the help-desk at the finger-tips of each operator, the quality of the support increases and hard- and software downtime decreases. The repository can also be used to analyze the recurrence of problems to determine weak spots in hard- and software, as well as to check what to prepare for during updates or migration. Once operators' experiences have been captured, the experiences can also be transferred among various sites of DaimlerChrysler worldwide. This ensures the same high standards of quality at every location.

The knowledge repository that contains the experience of the help-desk operators, as well as the tools to access this knowledge, must be easy to create, maintain, and update. Consistency, usability, and validity are essential. Creating and maintaining a model-based system of such a complex domain is impossible. Obviously, a rule-based, expert system approach is also bound to fail. Since

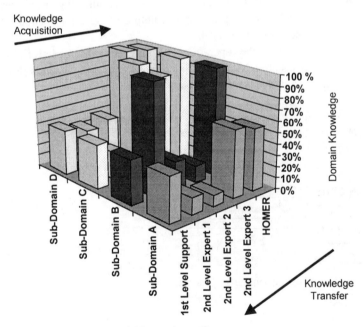

**Fig. 3.3.** Knowledge acquisition and transfer.

solutions in the form of cases do exist, and because of the obvious advantages in terms of ease of maintenance, the CBR approach was chosen for HOMER, the case-based help-desk support tool (*Ho*tline *mit E*rfahrung – Hotline with experience).

To estimate the financial gains that could be achieved by supporting the help-desk with a case-based system, we based our calculation on the calls that required more than 10 minutes and less than one day to solve. We assumed that the operators would not use the system for trivial calls (fewer than 10 minutes) and that problems that took longer than one day to solve required new hardware or software. Our calculations showed that the project would cover its costs if we managed to reduce the average time needed to answer a call by 50% for 40% of the incoming calls, i.e., if 60% of the calls were solved in the same time and 40% were solved in half the time.

The initial tests surpassed our expectations. With the initial case base, HOMER enabled the help-desk operators to solve 32% of the relevant calls in 6% of the time. The average time needed to solve a problem with HOMER was 9 minutes as opposed to 141 minutes with conventional methods (see section 3.1.8).

### 3.1.4 Knowledge Representation

To perform the initial test, printer-plotter problems were selected as the target domain and the second-level help-desk as the target user-group. Both the user-interface and the knowledge representation were developed accordingly.

When we started system development, representing the domain in a flat list of attribute value pairs or putting the experience of the operators in a textual, question-answer-oriented case base was very tempting (c.f. Thomas et. al. 97). Since the modeling effort would be low, the operators could enter cases themselves, and knowledge acquisition could proceed swiftly.

However, we soon realized that the cost of this "shallow" approach was the maintenance effort the company would need to put into the case base after it reached a certain size. Since the system had very limited knowledge about the structure and semantics of the domain, it could not aid in structuring the cases.

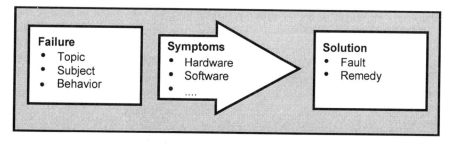

**Fig. 3.4.** Basic structure of a help-desk case.

Similarity calculation in such systems is based purely on surface features: the number of identical answers to questions or textual pattern matching of the cases. We therefore decided to use a structured, object-oriented approach to model the domain. Even if the effort necessary to create such a model was higher in the beginning, in the long run it is easier to maintain in complex domains. We also found the model very useful in guiding the help-desk operators while they described and entered cases, and during similarity calculation.

The cases in the help-desk domain were modeled based on the approach the help-desk operators use to solve problems (Fig. 3.4). The first thing a help-desk operator has is the *Failure* description given by an end- user. This description is a subjective description and may or may not have something to do with the actual cause of the problem. *Failure* in the case model comprises

- *the Topic*: the area in which the problem is located (hardware, software, network, printing, and so on),
- *the Subject*: the entity that the failure is related to (specific software, printer, screen, and so on),
- *the Behavior*: the way the subject (miss-) behaves (crashes, wrong print size, screeching sound, and so on).

The *Symptoms* are groups of attribute-value pairs that help the help-desk operator diagnose the fault. The symptoms contain the minimum amount of information necessary to diagnose the problem.

The *Solution* contains the *Fault*, i.e., what the cause of the problem was, and the *Remedy*, i.e., how to solve the problem. In the actual implementation of the system there is also some administrative information regarding the specifications needed to apply this remedy and how long it takes to solve the problem.

Each failure description can be the result of various symptoms, which in turn can be the result of various faults, which can be solved by applying various remedies. Every complete path from a failure to a solution is a case in our system.

### 3.1.5 The HOMER System

**The CBRWorks Server.** Domain modeling, case and model maintenance, and initial case acquisition is done using the *CBRWorks Server,* a tool developed by TECINNO. Because CBRWorks is written in Smalltalk, it is hardware independent. The system at DaimlerChrysler currently runs on a Windows NT machine. The *CBR-Works Server* stores the model and the case base and provides the tools that the administrator needs to model and maintain the domain.

Fig. 3.5 shows a snapshot of a small part of the domain model of HOMER. The tree-view on the left displays the hierarchical structure of the domain concepts. We have selected the *HelpDeskCase* to show the attribute slots.

The slot *Problem* contains a concept *Cproblem*, which describes the failure as mentioned above. *Situation* describes the symptoms. These are structured in sub-concepts to ease the maintenance of the domain model and to speed up the retrieval process. *Loesung* holds the solution to the given problem and *Administrativa* stores organizational and statistical information. *Loesung* and *Administrativa* are not *Discriminant*, i.e., these slots are not taken into account during similarity calculation.

The cases are stored in two areas: the *case buffer* and the actual *case base*. The case buffer stores the newly created cases that have not yet been confirmed. The confirmed cases reside in the main case base. The help-desk operator has the choice of restricting the search to the confirmed cases or of using the case buffer as well.

**The HOMER-Client.** The *HOMER-Client* is the interface for case retrieval, case acquisition and, case browsing to the *CBRWorks Server* and was written in Java. Earlier versions were developed as HTML-pages and later with JavaScript, but the dynamics and complexity of the domain model made development with these tools infeasible. Java was chosen because of its networking capabilities and the ease of making it available to the help-desk operator through a web server.

The HOMER-Client gives the operator all relevant information he/she needs in an easily understandable manner at one glance (Fig. 3.6). It assists the operator with two modes of execution.

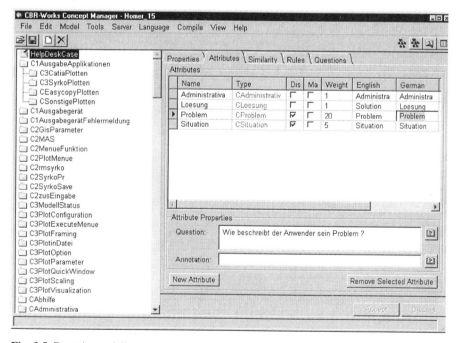

**Fig. 3.5.** Domain modeling.

In a *user-driven mode* the operator can build a query based on the domain model. This mode is meant for the experienced help-desk operator who does not need guidance on what to ask, knows the case structure, and wants to enter the data directly. The operator enters the query by selecting and specifying the relevant attributes in the domain structure shown in the tree view on the left side. This tree view can be switched off if the operator wants to go into the *system-driven mode*.

For the operator with less experience or the operator who wants support in what to ask, he/she can switch to the *system-driven mode*. In this mode the help-desk tool presents the most relevant questions to the operator. The tool generates the questions by selecting the attributes with the highest information gain based on the current case base. The help-desk operator can choose which question to ask the end user from the list at the top of the left side of the screen (Fig. 3.6).

The second list on the right side displays already-answered questions and the corresponding values in the most similar cases. The list on the bottom of the screen shows the suggested solutions in the order of relevance. The help-desk operator can view these in the case-browser by double-clicking them.

If the system cannot find an appropriate solution in the case base and the operator solves the problem in the conventional way, he/she enters this solution

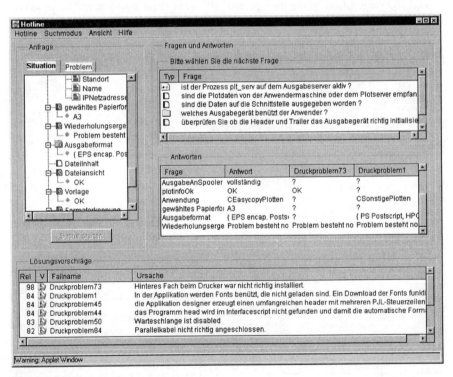

**Fig. 3.6.** The help-desk tool.

into the system and stores it, along with the query (problem and situation description) and administrative information, as a new case. The new case is stored in the case-buffer and later examined by the case-base editor (see section 3.1.6).

**System Architecture.** To ensure every help-desk operator accesses the same, up-to-date case base from every point in the network, the system is implemented using a client-server architecture. This enables us to use one central domain model and case base. The domain model and case-base are also easier to maintain.

Figure 3.7 shows the main components of the system. The *HOMER Clients* access the *CBRWorks Server* through the high bandwidth intranet of DaimlerChrysler. In terms of client-server systems, the *HOMER Client* is a *fat* client. It loads the whole domain model on start-up. Based on the domain model, it can build up queries as well as cases, and sends requests to the server only when needed. This obviously reduces network traffic. The communication language used

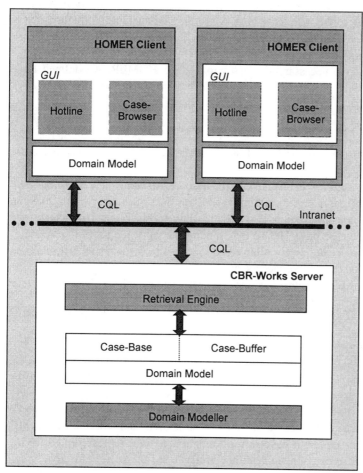

**Fig. 3.7.** System architecture.

is CQL (case query language), which was derived from CASUEL (Manago et al. 94), a query language developed in the INRECA project (Althoff et. al. 95).

### 3.1.6 Users and Roles

The complexity and size of the domain, as well as the demanded accuracy and consistency of the captured and reused experience, require the implementation of processes for case modeling, case acquisition, case maintenance, and case review.

As mentioned above, the case base is separated into a case-buffer and a main case base. The main case base contains reviewed, prototypical cases. The experience in the main case base represents the approved way of solving problems for the CAD/CAM help-desk. The case buffer contains the cases that were created by the help-desk operators during their daily work. These cases may or may not be worth transferring to the main case base. Since they do contain information that is relevant to the daily operation of the help-desk, they are available to all help-desk operators but marked as being "unconfirmed."

To implement the necessary processes to operate HOMER, we defined three user types: the *System Administrator*, the *Case Base Editor* and the *Help-Desk Operator*.

The *Help-Desk Operator* has the lowest access rights in the system. He/she is the person that uses HOMER on a daily basis to solve the problems of the end-users. The main tasks of the help-desk operator are *case-acquisition* and *case-retrieval*.

The *Case Base Editor* is responsible for *case maintenance* and *case approval*. He/she checks the cases in the case buffer and transfers relevant cases to the main case base. The case-base editor also has the duty to check for redundancy and consistency in the case base. He/she may modify the value ranges of the attributes in the domain model but is not allowed to modify the domain model itself (i.e., add/remove attributes, move concepts, and so on).

The *System Administrator* has the highest access rights. He/she performs *domain model maintenance* as well as *user-administration*.

### 3.1.7 Lessons Learned

**Technical Issues.** The design and layout of the user interface turned out to be essential in the development of the system and its acceptance by the help-desk operators. Even though the help-desk operators are experienced computer users, they want the user interface to be clearly structured and not inundated with information. They prefer to have less information on one screen then to having everything on the screen at once, and they prefer to switch to the respective screen whenever they need structural or more detailed information.

The help-desk operators use the cases that have been retrieved along with the suggested questions as guides while solving problems. Case focusing and question reordering based on information gain are perceived as very useful features in the help-desk system.

In situations where the system cannot retrieve a solution, the help-desk operators use the structured domain model as a guide while solving the problem. The domain model also allows us to make reliable similarity calculations and support the help-desk operator during case-entry.

**Organizational Issues.** Knowledge acquisition has been (and is) much more time consuming than we expected in the beginning. There are three main reasons for this: The help-desk operators have little time to spare from their operational duties, they are inexperienced in formulating their knowledge, and we want the resulting case base to contain prototypical cases that are accurate and consistent. When we started the project, we thought that we could use the 17,000 trouble-tickets that had been stored for the last years as cases. We soon found that these lacked essential information and were useless (except for reminding the help-desk operators what else they had to take into account).

A CBR system is a means of storing, sharing and reusing experience. If the experience stored in a CBR system is used only by the person who enters it, the system's usefulness will be limited. The goal of a CBR system is to create a experience repository that can be used and filled by a group of people. However, as soon as a system is being used by a user-group, maintenance processes have to be put into place, and tasks and responsibilities have to be defined. We discovered that it is important to put the processes for system maintenance in place as soon as possible. These tasks have to be performed by dedicated personnel.

**Managerial Issues.** An aspect that is often neglected, but which we found crucial to the project's success, is involving a corporation's management in the specification, development, and utilization of a system. Since a knowledge repository is only as good as the quality of the knowledge contained within it, continuous maintenance is necessary. This, however, requires effort and must be approved by management. By ensuring that management is involved and informed during the specification and development processes, awareness can be created, motivation can be kept high, and continuos support can be achieved.

### 3.1.8  Results Achieved

After initial knowledge acquisition in HOMER was finished, the system was put to the test at the second-level, printer-plotter help-desk in Sindelfingen. For two months, incoming calls were monitored and, depending on their applicability, solved with HOMER.

Since we did not want to interfere with the normal operation of the help-desk and the end-users, we decided to have the help-desk operator first solve the problem in a conventional manner. After the call had been resolved, the operator solved the same problem using HOMER. If no solution was found, the case was entered as a new case into the case base.

During the two month test period, 102 calls were handled by the second-level help-desk operator who performed the test. Forty-five of these calls were either trivial, directed to the wrong help-desk, or could not be reproduced (the failure disappeared). Of the remaining 57 problems, HOMER solved 18 (i.e., 32%). While the average problem resolution time for these problems was 141 minutes without HOMER, the help-desk operator needed only 9 minutes on average to solve problems with HOMER. This result was much better than what we based our calculations on when the project was initiated.

As a next step, HOMER and the printer-plotter case base are being transferred to another production site of DaimlerChrysler. This site is currently implementing the same process chain for their printer-plotter environment as was done in Sindelfingen. Since the help-desk operators as yet have no experience with the process chain, the printer-plotter cases in HOMER are of great value to them.

An interesting side-effect is that in the course of initial knowledge acquisition, the help-desk operators gained a much deeper insight into the processes involved in the domain that was being modeled. This resulted in several enhancements and has reduced the number of calls that arrive at the help-desk as well.

### 3.1.9 Summary

Using INRECA technology, DaimlerChrysler and TECINNO developed a system that stores the experience of the help-desk operators in a case base and enables them to access, reuse, and extend the knowledge in a natural and straightforward manner. The project allowed the experience of the help-desk operators to be gathered and preserved, ensuring that solutions to previous problems are available. Since the time needed to solve problems decreased drastically, the productivity of the supported departments increased.

Currently, the first version of HOMER, the Hotline with Experience, is operational at the second-level printer-plotter help-desk in Sindelfingen. Knowledge acquisition, as well as system development, are continuing. The system has also been used as a technology demonstrator to initiate several other help-desk projects at different locations of DaimlerChrysler.

## 3.2 A Case-Based Product Catalog of Operational Amplifiers

Analog Devices, Inc., (ADI) designs, manufactures, and markets a broad line of high-performance linear, mixed-signal, and digital integrated circuits (ICs) that address a wide range of real-world signal processing applications. Analog sells its products worldwide through a direct sales force, third-party industrial distributors, and independent sales representatives. The company has direct sales offices in 17 countries, including the United States. Founded in 1965, Analog Devices employs approximately 6,000 people worldwide. Many of Analog Device's customers are small electronics firms or electronics departments of large firms. A design engineer is the usual contact point with the central applications department. Analog Devices, at the time of building the application, employed up to 15 engineers to provide applications support to their customers and potential customers. The engineer takes the customer's requirements for a product over the phone and tries to find a match in the AD product range. This process can involve weighing up dozens of constraints while at the same time interacting with the customer to get an assessment of the customer's priorities. Engineers handle about 40 calls per day, 50% of which relate to product selection. The remaining 50% relate to technical support in the use of a specific product.

In 1997, ADI decided to support the customer consultation process using a CBR system. The application development focused initially on *operational amplifiers*, a product category within the Analog Devices product catalogue. Analog Devices has over 130 operational amplifiers in its catalog, each one specified by up to 40 parameters. Parameters can be real, integer, symbolic, or Boolean. Of the 40 parameters 39 require specific similarity search functions so that a requested value can be compared to the value of a specific operational amplifier in the case base. Since the first application to operational amplifiers, ADI with support form Interactive Multimedia Systems has applied the same technology to its Analog to Digital (ADC) and Digital to Analog (DAC) converters.

A number of issues brought Analog Devices to the point where it wanted to provide a computer-based service to its customers. One of these was the cost of field-applications support engineers. At issue was not just the cost of salaries but also the cost of training a person to the skill level he or she needed to match a product to a customer's requirement. In addition, a fixed number of engineers can only provide service to a fixed number of customers. The need to cover multiple time zones further diluted this scarce resource. Although it is difficult to picture customer requirements over the phone, the log from a parametric search facility presents a very valuable picture of customer requirements. This resource can then act as direct input into the product design, marketing, and production planning. The solution to the problem was to provide the customer with access to an intelligent search facility based on the INRECA nearest-neighbor matching functionality. The facility allows customers to specify their requirements interactively with the parametric search software. A customer can specify cut-off values for most parameters, can optimize all parameters, and can assign priority to any parameter. In return for specifying parametric values, the customer gets a list of the top 10 products in the Analog Devices range that are closest to meeting his or her specified requirements. The customer can then link directly to the detailed data sheet for individual products. The customer can further specify or refine the parametric search until he or she finds the solution that meets all requirements. Analog Device's competitors in the market place all offer some form of search capability over the Internet, but in every case the parameters are restricted to a selection of part number, product category, price, and possibly one other parameter. These other search facilities restrict the customer to one or two meaningful parameters or otherwise require that the customer knows the product before starting the search.

### 3.2.1 The Application Development Process

The first phase of the development process involved gathering requirements for the application through interviews with technical and business staff from ADI. This step required about four meetings in total followed by analysis of the discussions. From this, during a period of four weeks, software developers prepared separate search- and user-interface demonstrations. ADI provided us with detailed feedback on these separate demonstrations and this input was used to create the engineered and integrated application. The first application took, in total, six months to produce and involved about 15 analyst days and about 35 developer days. The second application took fewer than six weeks and the third application fewer than 10 days. These savings were possible, by in large, by the automation of certain steps in the process.

### 3.2.2 Benefit Analysis

Analysis of the project one year later allows us to list the following benefits related to the use of an intelligent parametric search facility.

#### For the Customer

- The customer has full flexibility and the opportunity to "negotiate" with the system in order to select a product. The customer can do this using all 40+ parameters of the device.
- The service short cuts the normal research activity and, therefore, reduces testing, design, and direct search costs for the customer.
- The search engine provides an immediate equivalents list, which can save significant time in research and gives greater flexibility at the production stage.

- The parametric search facility always returns a solution, unlike traditional SQL-style searches, which only return a value if all conditions are exactly met.
- The facility offers a selection of alternatives, just as an engineer or sales person might.

**For the Manufacturer**

- The service frees up the experienced field-applications engineers, allowing them to spend more time addressing complex customer-support requirements.
- The service leads to greater product sales at the product-design phase (by supporting engineers), and this implies greater sales at the production phase.
- A valuable source of marketing information is generated when the customer specifies his application requirements to the parametric search facility. The information can provide input into the design and production of the products.
- The service is better than anything available and therefore will improve the image of the manufacturer. This progressive image should result in increased product listings by distributors.
- The manufacturer gets to know his customer better and can use the information gathered by the search engine to target promotional materials to specific customers and to tailor other services to customer needs

### 3.2.3 Similarity Functions Used in the Application

The Analog Devices application is in a technical domain where high-exponent values for individual parameters are normal. Values can go down to $10^{-18}$ and up to $10^{12}$. This makes calculating similarity to the correct precision a real challenge. We therefore set about defining similarity functions that met the requirements of this technical domain. We list the key approaches below.

**Similarity Calculation for Numerical Parameters.** The similarity calculation for "less is better" is shown in Fig. 3.8. The similarity calculation for "more is better" is simply a mirror image of this "less is better" graph. The step from 1.0 to 0.5 is necessary to sufficiently differentiate between values that just meet the cut-off and those that just miss the cut-off. The cut-off when specified by the user is very important and must influence the search.

**Similarity Search for Model Number.** The search engine allows searching by model number. The model number is an alpha-numeric with between four and ten characters. The following is the similarity search function for model number.

- Example: Query value = OP?62: Any model number for which the only different character is that specified by "?" returns a value of 1; all others return a value of 0.

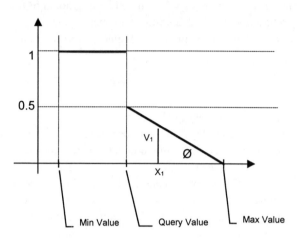

**Fig. 3.8.** "Less is better" similarity graph: any case value less than or equal to the query value returns a value of "1". Any case value greater than the query function returns a value calculated by the following: $V_1 = 0.5 *[(max - X_1) / (max - query)]$.

- Example: Query value = AD8*: Any model number for which the first characters are the same as those coming before the "*" returns 1; all others return 0.
- Example Query value = AD7580: Only the model number that matches the query exactly returns 1; all others return 0.
- It is possible to combine the previous examples in a comma-separated list. Example: Query value = OP?3, AD75*, OP34.

### 3.2.4 How the Software Works

**Searching.** A requirement for a specific product is expressed in terms of the desired parameters for that product (see Fig. 3.9 and 3.10). The parameters are organized into groupings that can be selected by clicking on the appropriate tab. The groupings that apply to Op Amps are DYNAMIC, INPUT, OUTPUT, SUPPLY, OTHER, and SPECIAL. Much the same groupings would apply to other categories of electronic devices; however, the parameter list would be quite different.

For any numerical parameter, the user can enter a cutoff or type "best," but not both. For any non-numerical parameter, the user can either select a value from a list or type a desired value. For any parameter, the user can check "priority." For any parameter without optimize (best) (generally non-numerical parameters), the user can select "priority" only AFTER a desired value (or cutoff) has been entered. Numerical values can include a place-holder suffix. The first letter following a number entered by the user is interpreted on the server side to signify a unit for the value entered. (e.g. 9.9E3=9900). Clicking on any parameter abbreviation will link to a complete description of that parameter. RESET will clear all entered data from all parameters.

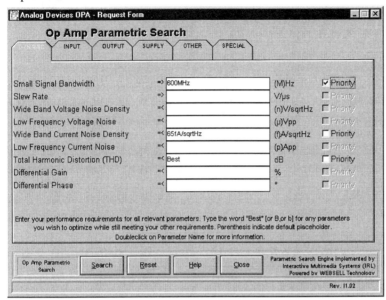

**Fig. 3.9.** Query screen for Op Amps product search (DYNAMIC).

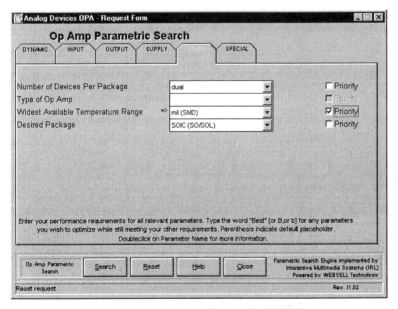

**Fig. 3.10.** Query screen for Op Amps product search (OTHER).

If a parameter has a "=>" symbol to the left of the data-entry field, this means that the value selected or entered by the user is to be interpreted as "more is best" or more properly "greater than or equal to is best." This indication does not, however, exclude products that might have a lower value for this parameter but meet all other requirements. It thus avoids the problem of the near miss in which a product that matches all but one of the requirements is not returned by a normal database search.

**Results.** The search procedure is almost instantaneous and when it is complete, the application hands the results over to the Results Display component of the software (see Fig. 3.11 and 3.12). The resulting product specifications are displayed in two groups of five ordered by their similarity with the user's requirements. From here, clicking on any part number takes the user to the data sheet of that part, which appears as a PDF document in Adobe Acrobat Exchange. Clicking on the NEW SEARCH button will take the user back to the Query screen. "Optimize" under the request column indicates that the user specified "best" in the query page. An "!" after a value in the request column indicates that the user decided to select this parameter. Any value in the results column that fails to meet the user's request is shown in red. If one or more values fail for a given product, the "Part Number" at the top of the column is shown in red. The "Hold" checkbox at the top of each column allows the user to store this part in the Selected Devices list.

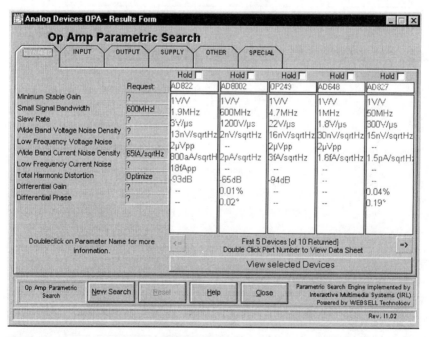

**Fig. 3.11.** Results display (DYNAMIC).

In Fig. 3.12 three of the symbolic parameters have values selected, one with a priority. The assessment of whether a value meets a requirement is different for each of these parameters. For *number of devices per package*, the similarity is calculated based on a matrix with a value ranging from (0.0 to 1.0) specified for each cell in the matrix. In the case of *temperature range*, the approach is different as this is an ordered symbol. Here in the AD8002, temperature range with value *industrial* is lower than *mil(SMD)* in the ordered list and therefore fails to meet the requirement. Thus it returns a similarity of ~0.6 and appears in red.  The OP249 has a temperature range with value *mil(space)*, which is higher than *mil(SMD)* in the ordered list and thus returns a similarity of 1.0 and appears black. *Available packages* is specified as SOIC and returns a value of 1.0 if present in the list or 0.0 if not.

The individual similarities for each of these parameters are combined to give an overall measure of similarity for the part in question. This overall measure is weighted based on priorities selected by the user and is used to list the parts in order of closeness - all in a fraction of a second.

The user can elect to hold certain parts from the results of a given search and, over multiple searches, assemble a list of the parts he or she is interested in. The "Selected Devices" list allows the user to compare parts from multiple searches side by side and to print the full list if required (see Fig. 3.13).

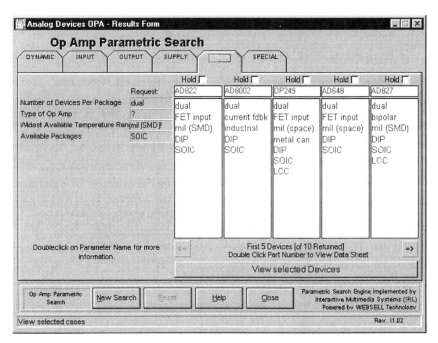

**Fig. 3.12.** Results display (OTHER).

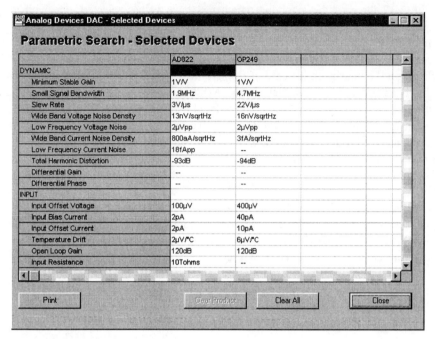

**Fig. 3.13.** Results held from an individual search.

### 3.2.5  Status of the Application

To date, the Analog Devices parametric search system has been delivered twice on CD-ROM to over 100,000 customers worldwide and has been available on the company's Intranet for engineers. At the time of this writing, the equivalent functionality available on the CD-ROM is being prepared for the company's web site. This is expected to be available in the summer of 1999. Reactions from ADI customers have been consistently positive, and the service has clearly distinguished ADI as a pioneer in the production of an intelligent product catalog for electronic devices. The INRECA methodology allowed the CBR application developers at IMS to routinely build additional catalog search applications based on the methods developed during the Analog Devices projects. Since then, IMS has focussed on automating steps in the application-development process, allowing them to deliver applications quickly and pass on savings to their customers.

## 3.3 Case-Based Maintenance Support for TGV Trains

### 3.3.1 TGV's Environment

Introduced by the French railway operator SNCF in 1981, the very high speed train TGV connects Paris and Lyon (550 km). Other lines were opened starting in 1989 with the TGV Atlantique which has a rated speed of 300 km/h. The Eurostar connects France, England and Belgium through the channel tunnel, and the TGV Thalyss connects France, Belgium, Holland and Germany. The TGV offers best performance with a superior life cycle cost gain in terms of traction, performance, reliability, maintainability, availability and passenger comfort and safety.

One of the key factors in reducing vehicle operation costs is to increase the vehicle availability, which means improving vehicle reliability and accelerating diagnostics when the vehicles break down.

To create a new computer-aided maintenance system, several technologies were considered for developing a reliable and evolutionary diagnostic tool: expert systems, Case-Based Reasoning, and model-based reasoning. A combination of structural Case-Based Reasoning and inductive techniques was finally chosen.

### 3.3.2 A Hierarchy of Data Models and Case Bases

Being able to create a diagnostic system that is flexible and capable of enriching its own knowledge base over time were key factors for selecting a combination of CBR and inductive techniques. The problem of case-base maintenance is critical in this application. Indeed, any major module of a train can be hierarchically decomposed into subsystems, or minor modules. However, these subsystems are often linked to one another. Difficulties arise when the model changes. For example, let us suppose that the state of a relay is added to the case model to differentiate two types of problem that affect a subsystem. This change has an impact over all the cases, including the ones that are on a different subsystems. A new attribute has to be added to the other subsystems. However, the service technicians cannot invest the effort to go back to fill the attribute value for these other cases. Thus, the attribute is unknown in all cases that are located in these other subsystems. Unfortunately, this high rate of unknown values creates problems for both the induction and the dynamic induction. For instance, for induction, the same subtrees are repeated over and over again in different parts of the decision tree. The decision tree is, therefore, difficult to validate and to maintain for the application developer, and harder to use for the service technician.

Thus, a single model and a single case base are not easy to create, validate, and maintain. The technical solution chosen was to break down the model that describes the all the equipment into hierarchically ordered submodels that describe subsystems of the equipment. In parallel, the case bases are broken down into smaller chunks. A top-level case base aims at identifying the final diagnostic OR points at another subcase base, and so on. When a subcase base is modified, this only has a local effect and does not create problems for other case bases. However, an attribute (e.g., start of relay xyz) can be shared among several case bases, and the system must inherit the state of the relay from a higher-level case base if it is required lower in the hierarchy.

Figure 3.14 displays a subpart of the model hierarchy for the equipment called "chain of traction" (this includes the engine, the brakes, the alimentation, and so on), which is characterized by a set of fault codes called "30/40." Note that, for instance, the submodel "CHQQT43" and, thus, the corresponding subcase base, appears seven times in this hierarchy.

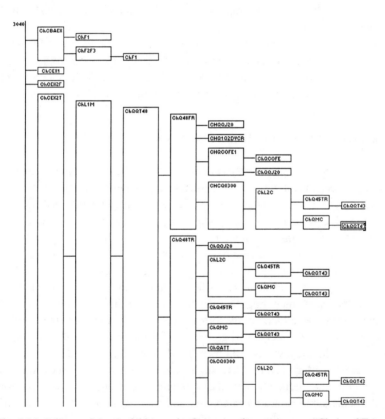

**Fig. 3.14.** Subpart of the model hierarchy for a complex equipment "Chain of Traction".

Each submodel that appears in this hierarchy is very simple (fewer than 15 attributes on average). Each subcase base is limited, on average, to 30 cases. Figure 3.15 displays the data model related to submodel "CHQQT43."

### 3.3.3 Technical Approach for Diagnosis

The diagnostic runs in two phases:

1. A depth-first approach is proposed first, which quickly guides the technician towards the most probable faulty subequipment. This is achieved through an

```
3040
  Modele1 LRU0 (S)
    0
  BASENAME (S)
  Elément déposable (S)
    QQT43
    QT43
    L2M
    L1
    L1C
    L2
    CEX1
    CEX2
    CBAEX
    L1M
    F1
    F3
    F2
  Tension 101P/101Q sur QQT43 (S)
    72
    0
  Tension 101CK sur QT43 (S)
    72
    0
  Tension 101N sur L2M (S)
    72
    0
  Tension 101M sur L1 (S)
    72
    0
  Tension 101L sur L1C (S)
    72
    0
  Tension 101K sur L2 (S)
    72
    0
  Tension 101J sur CEX1 (S)
    72
    0
  Tension 101H sur CEX2 (S)
    72
    0
  Tension 101F sur CBAEX (S)
    72
    0
  Tension 101D sur L1M (S)
    72
    0
  Tension 101C sur F1 (S)
    72
    0
  Tension 101B sur F3 (S)
    72
    0
```

**Fig. 3.15.** Submodel CHQQT43. Most of the attributes are Boolean with values "0" and "72" (this represents a voltage measure). "Elément déposable" contains the list of LRUs: QQT43, QT43, and so on (relays, cards, etc.). The case base that corresponds to this data model contains only 13 cases.

induction process. The system uses either fault trees that have been previously generated in each case base or dynamic induction where the most relevant questions are dynamically generated. When the system proposes navigating into several different case bases, the technician must decide the most accurate choice. This process is repeated in the hierarchy of case bases until the user obtains a diagnosis.

2. At the end of the induction phase, a CBR query is fired to see if another problem, whose fault signature is similar, can be found, possibly in different subcase bases. The query case has to be reconstituted from the different levels in the hierarchy. The process is fairly complicated from a technical standpoint (it is documented in a process diagram in section 9.2.3,) but it works.

### 3.3.4 Example of the System in Action

We present now an example of how the system is used for diagnostic support of the TGV on-board computer network. While a TGV is in circulation, its embedded electronics equipment continually receives data about the train's functions. Each car of the TGV has an on-board controller, which communicates through a dual network with the on-board controllers of the other cars (and even with the cars of another TGV when they are in duplex mode). These controllers are in charge of temperature control, doors control, light control, and so on. To monitor the correctness of the communication within the network, each controller provides some information about the data it receives and sends: Percentage of inactivity, percentage of lost information, and so on. When these percentages reach some predefined thresholds, alarms are propagated through the network. All this information is logged into batch files, which can be transmitted in real time to the maintenance center or analyzed latter. Figure 3.16 shows a display of the HTML interface that receives this information from the on-board computers.

From this synthesized information, the maintenance technician must decide which controller is faulty (because of the network connectivity, it is not always the one that displays the alarm), and what the fault is: bad wire connection, faulty card, and so on. As explained in the previous section, the maintenance technician must start the consultation process with the top-level case base, which describes the overall network. The diagnostic system guides him through the case base hierarchy towards the correct LRU (a card, a wire, or something else) he must check. If the check is correct, he can enlarge the search to other LRUs in other case bases by starting the CBR search.

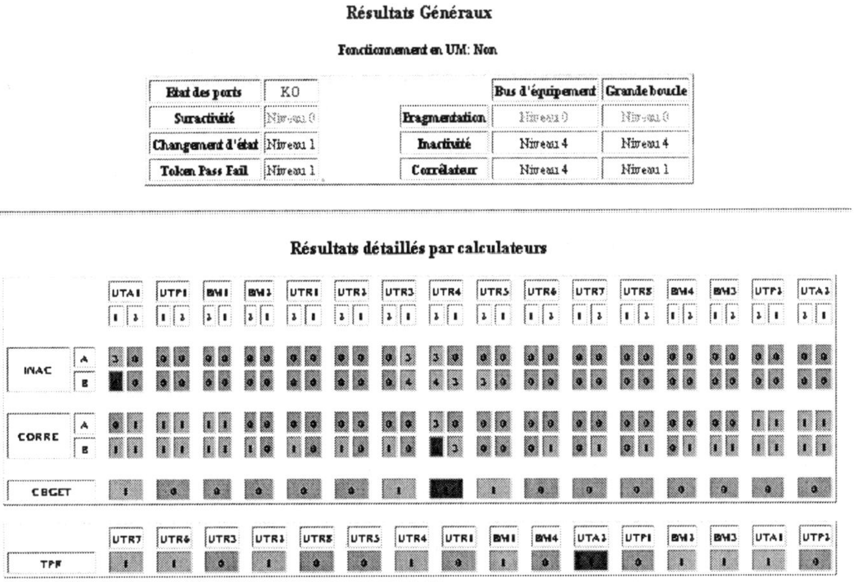

**Résultats Généraux**

Fonctionnement en UM: Non

| Etat des ports | KO | | Bus d'équipement | Grande boucle |
|---|---|---|---|---|
| Suractivité | Niveau 0 | Fragmentation | Niveau 0 | Niveau 0 |
| Changement d'état | Niveau 1 | Inactivité | Niveau 4 | Niveau 4 |
| Token Pass Fail | Niveau 1 | Corrélateur | Niveau 4 | Niveau 1 |

**Résultats détaillés par calculateurs**

Fig. 3.16. Data transferred from the TGV for on-board network analysis.

## 3.3.5  Integration into the End-User Environment

The diagnostic tool is not used alone by the maintenance technicians, but as part of a larger information management system. The end-user has access to this information-management system through a Internet/Intranet link to the application server. Thus, at this phase we plan the link among the databases of the maintenance platform. This includes the equipment databases (and the train itself), the historical databases, and the technical documentation:

– Information retrieval in the equipment database with respect to a parameter required by the diagnostic tool (technical documentation, images, parts catalog, and so on). This retrieval is based on a common indexing scheme between the data models used by the diagnostic tool and the databases of the maintenance platform.
– Information retrieval in the train database with respect to a parameter required by the diagnostic tool (state of a relay, position of a door, and so on). The diagnostic tool can send a request to the train database to receive and exploit the answer. The communication is based on the TCP/IP protocol.

Figure 3.17 depicts roughly the links between the diagnostic tool and the various databases.

- The diagnostic tool uses HTML interfaces for the end-users, allowing them to access the central web server. It proposes a series of actions and simple questions (type of answer should be yes/no). It is possible to directly access the equipment data and/or the historical data known on the considered equipment. All the end-user's actions are logged into a report file, which allows them to be analyzed off-line for data models and for updating case bases.
- The diagnostic tool also includes specialized interfaces for the specialists in charge of managing the data bases: modification of the data models and of the model hierarchy, creation of analytical cases, validation of new cases created by the technicians of the after-sales service, analysis of the log reports, and so on. These processes are documented in process diagrams in chapter 9 (see sections 9.2.1 and 9.2.2).

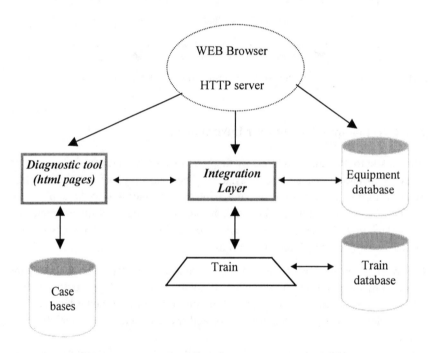

**Fig. 3.17.** Communication between the diagnostic tool and the databases.

### 3.3.6  Status of the Application

The diagnostic tool is now being scaled up for use on portable PCs and on an Intranet. The tool will then be used 24 hours a day by transportation operators' maintenance crews.

# Part II

# Developing Case-Based Application with the INRECA Methodology

This second part of the book, which consists of the chapter 4 through 6, explains in detail the core of the INRECA methodology. We explain how a CBR system is developed and how development experience is captured, documented, and reused to enable effective and successful CBR projects.

**Chapter 4** "Practical Guidelines for Developing Case-Based Reasoning Applications" introduces the general steps that occur in almost every CBR project. It focuses on practical managerial aspects.

**Chapter 5** "Professional Case-Based Reasoning Application Development" introduces the foundations of the INRECA methodology, which are essential for cost-efficient CBR application development.

**Chapters 6** "Documenting Case-Based Reasoning Development Experience" describes in detail how to use software process models to structure and document CBR development projects and how to use the INRECA methodology tool to publish this experience on an Intranet or the Internet to enable efficient project planning.

# 4. Practical Guidelines for Developing Case-Based Reasoning Applications

Since the first commercial CBR applications in the early '90'-s a number of examples of successful deployments of CBR have contributed to the practical experience with this technology. This chapter gives an introduction to those aspects that need to be considered during planning, implementation, and actually running a CBR system. It is a nine-step path towards the long-term success of CBR applications (see figure below). The INRECA methodology for building CBR applications, introduced in the subsequent chapters of this book, gives detailed descriptions and guidance on how to enact these steps. The view presented within this chapter focuses on the practical managerial aspects.

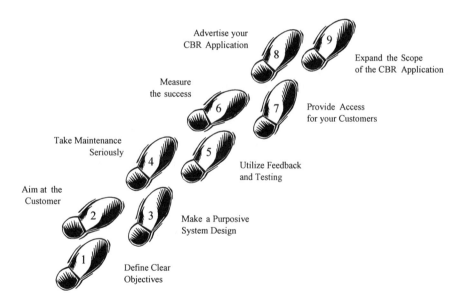

## 4.1 Define Your Measures of Success

*As in almost every software project, you should formulate clear objectives and measures of success.*

Each project requires well-defined measures of success for its execution. Our experiences with many projects have shown us that the clearer the objectives, the greater the quality of the results and the project's success. The impact of such measures is twofold:

1. There is a unique goal for the project team that focuses the teamwork from the beginning onwards, all team members having a common understanding of the planned results.
2. The management can control the project: problems and deviations from the project plan can be observed early and contingency plans deployed effectively.

Many of today's knowledge-management projects still have very fuzzy objectives, such as "improve the capture and re-use of the available corporate knowledge". In practice, it is impossible to measure success against a vague goal like this, which prevents control. A well-defined objective provides quantifiable, or at least observable, qualitative measurements, which allow monitoring and control of the project.

As Philip Klahr, Vice President of Inference, said: *"The real question to pose is: What is the single most important thing this knowledge base must do for management to call it successful?"*

There are many and sometimes conflicting objectives that have been targeted by different CBR projects. The following list summarises some of these goals of CBR systems (the examples have been chosen from different types of applications, such as help-desks, call-center support, diagnosis, and catalog search):

- improve the quality and consistency of responses to customers,
- improve customer as well as employee satisfaction,
- reduce the time, and therefore the cost, of solving a customer problem,
- reduce the cost-per-customer interaction,
- solve the customer's problem during the first contact,
- reduce cost by freeing experts from routine tasks,
- reduce the number of inquiries that need to be escalated to the second level support,
- optimize employee training,
- standardize customer interaction,
- improve control of customer support,
- improve flexibility of staffing,
- increase self-servicing,
- decrease number of appointments for service technicians,
- improve efficiency of the service organization,

- reduced cost of catalog distribution by online catalogs,
- reduce routine work of customer consultants with intelligent CBR catalogs,
- ensure the customer always receives an offer; CBR catalogs always make an offer.

All the above objectives have been met by successful CBR systems; however, they sometimes compete with each other in practice. For example, "reducing the cost per call at a hotline help-desk by reducing the call duration" contradicts with the objective "to handle more complex problems directly during the first contact by the hotline operators."

Consequently, the design of a CBR system for a quick call handling at the hotline will differ from the one that is designed to solve as many problems as possible. Similar examples can be found in all other application areas. This, again, stresses the need to formulate goals and objectives as precisely as possible. These goals should be realistic and measurable, i.e., enable previous and subsequent stages to be compared.

**Rule of Thumb:** Be as clear and relevant as possible when defining the objectives of your CBR system.


## 4.2  Orient Your Customers

*You must understand your customers and your users.*

A knowledge-based application is successful if it fulfills the requirements and expectations of its users. It must respect the experience and technical knowledge of its users, as well as their diagnostic and analytical competence.

Here, the term "user" or "customer" refers to everyone who actually uses the application, including both clients and call-center agents. Since they all consume the services offered by the system, they all should be viewed as customers. However the "real" customer, or client, is the most important one. The performance of both after-sales service and the sales force primarily benefits the customer.

The inexperienced user needs step-by-step guidance throughout the problem-solving process, while the experienced one prefers instant access to the solution.

In some cases it may be additionally necessary to take the language and cultural background of the user into consideration. For example, the American user usually likes to play around with a software system while the English user does not, even though they speak the same language. Furthermore, in different cultures the same term may have a different meaning.

You cannot expect the client to be familiar with corporate terminology. Usually, he or she does not know the identification numbers of parts or goods. In the case of a troubleshooting procedure he or she will need help and support during the capture of the required information.

Also, legal aspects influence the application design. For reasons of security, for example it is not sufficient to request that a customer opens the casing of an electrical device to check the voltage of the power supply. Similarly, you would not ask explicitly for the password of an online customer, even if it is the cause for his logon problem. The right question might be whether she or he has used some special characters for his password.

Case base design must enable the successful use of the system by all intended users. It should encourage them to trust the proposed solutions, both at present and in the future. This affects the querying of required information as well as the presentation of the results. Whether an application is accepted by its users strongly depends on whether it is understood by the target user groups, which should be motivated to use the system.

In many cases, different target groups will use the same case base. However, analysis reveals consultation with the system is initiated by the customer-user, regardless of whether it is a self-service application or a call-center that handles customer's problems. This implies that the design of the case base is ruled by the customer's needs and terminology, and that it is the customer who benefits from the results.

**Rule of Thumb:** You must consider the specific requirements, abilities, and restrictions of the primary users of the system – your coworkers and customers.


## 4.3  Get the Big Picture

*Foresee, during the early days of the system design, the context in which the final application will be deployed.*

During the first two steps we analyzed two key aspects that are decisive for the success of a CBR project:

1.  The definition of objectives and measures of success,
2.  The focus of attention on the expectations and abilities of the user.

Additional aspects arise from the circumstances and the surrounding where the system will be deployed: its context and purpose. This includes organizational, technical, and financial questions, for example, "Which requirements need to be derived from the integration of the system into the existing IT environment?" or "Which level of data security has to be reached?"

System integration may require the definition of interfaces with existing databases, for example, a call-tracking system, product-data management, or customer-data management system. These interfaces may even influence the design of the final application's user interfaces. If the system is to be deployed at a call-center as well as on the Internet or CD-ROM, then this has to be considered during the design, to avoid expensive redesigns during the lifetime of the system.

Knowledge of the domain itself must be covered as comprehensively as possible. This is a prerequisite for a viable domain model. Attributes and their ranges of value, as well as similarity measures and interrogation sequences, must be defined. The latter have a strong impact on the users' acceptance of the system.

To achieve an efficient and extendable CBR application, these aspects should already have been analyzed during the planning stage of the project. This ensures a long-term contribution by the CBR application to the corporate competitiveness. Therefore everyone involved in the planning, development, maintenance and use of the system must contribute to the design process. All design decisions should be documented (for example, as proposed in the methodology presented in this book) to ensure the consistency of the overall development process.

**Rule of Thumb:** Consider the organizational, technical, and financial constraints of the application from the very beginning and at all subsequent stages.

## 4.4  Think About Maintenance

*The benefits of a CBR application stand or fall on the content's topicality.*

Many companies succeeded through the first three steps – well-defined objectives, focus on the customer's needs, and purposive design – and quickly meet the measures of success they had set. But to stay successful in the long term, it is necessary to establish knowledge-management processes that ensure that the knowledge, as expressed in the case data and the domain model, is updated and maintained on a regular basis. This must be a commonly agreed corporate objective. In all cases where this task and effort were neglected, the investment into the system turned out to be a waste of money, since the application was outdated as quickly as it was set up.

Investing in the system's maintenance always pays back: If the experience and domain knowledge of the users increase, and this gain is not reflected in the CBR application then the quality of the results of the system will decrease, followed by a decrease in the users' satisfaction. Sooner or later they will start to boycott the system.

Outdated knowledge leads to frustration and disappointment. For instance, a travel broker must, of course, sell actually available flights and trips. What is obvious in this example is often neglected in practice. Maintaining the data base not only requires that new knowledge be added to the case base but that old cases be edited to keep them up to date. Almost all large companies employ someone who is responsible for their databases: The database system administrator. A similar role is required for knowledge administration, and many companies have created the position of a Chief Information Officer (CIO), thereby establishing this function at the top management level. The task of a CIO is to implement and operate a powerful knowledge-management process. You should define such an explicit process within your organization to ensure a regular knowledge update. The elements of such a process are:

1. The identification and capture of emerging corporate knowledge. New knowledge arises when new or additional products are introduced or when products are replaced. Such developments are reflected by new and extended lists of frequently-asked questions and new service reports, or simply by new product descriptions and catalogs. New knowledge also emerges when new problems are solved.
2. The newly captured knowledge needs to be integrated into the existing knowledge base: The case base and the domain model have to be updated.
3. The updated knowledge base has to be distributed to its users, when necessary, after localization (translation and adaptation to cultural particular).

Special attention should be paid to the solution of those problem cases that could not have been solved within the experience of the existing case base. These need to be dealt with quickly and fed back to the system, enhancing case base experience. Users will only trust the system when they observe regular updates of the system and when failures do not recur. In the case of self-service applications users repeatedly interrogate the system for unsolved problems to check whether it has been updated. They also check to see whether they are being taken seriously. This shows that if you cannot update your system immediately, you should at least include a notice that you are dealing with the topic.

**Rule of Thumb:** Knowledge management is a continuous process. Ensure that your case base and the domain model are up to date. Be prepared to extend the system with new functionality and for new application areas.

## 4.5  Welcome Feedback and Testing

*Benefit from user feedback.*

During the introduction of the CBR cycle in section 2.6, the importance of the revision stage was stressed. To measure the success of a CBR application in practice, encourage users to provide feedback, for example, whether the result the system provided was sufficient. A system's users are best suited to appraise its benefits.

Since in most cases it is not possible to completely cover a knowledge domain, a CBR application sometimes will produce incomplete or even wrong results. If such a situation occurs, the overall interrogation process should be traced, analyzed, and evaluated by an expert in the domain. In addition, within a call center, how a customer's request was solved (by intuition?) or further treated (by second-level support, call back, other?) should be recorded. This information can be used to improve the CBR application; it needs to be recognized as part of the overall knowledge-management process.

The above should be seen as an opportunity for optimization, rather than as a failure of the technology or the knowledge-management approach. During the development stage, with its more-or-less clean software laboratory conditions, it is hard to foresee all the eventualities that might occur in the real world with real customers. To improve the system, you must allow it to benefit from the customers' experiences in using it.

**Rule of Thumb:** Test your case bases and the CBR application. Use user feedback to continuously optimize your system.

## 4.6  Measure the Success

*Only well-defined measures of success ensure the long-term control of success.*

As with any project it is important to be in control of the success or failure of the CBR application. With CBR and knowledge-management projects in general the calculation of the ROI and the break-even point is hampered by lots of criteria that are difficult to measure. We need to differentiate between these soft criteria and the hard criteria that are quantifiable and can be evaluated monetarily.

During the introduction of a CBR application, the company usually estimates the cost of inaction. This is an estimation of the cost for personnel, administration, and so on, after the system is introduced (i.e., an estimation of the expected increase of efficiency with the CBR application) as compared to the cost without the system. These projected costs enable quite good estimations of the ROI and the break-even point. It is important to define a measure to evaluate the project's progress and success against the objectives and criteria that have been defined in the first step of the CBR application-building process, as described in section 4.1.

Often, companies do not continuously measure progress, or at least not against the defined criteria. Here it is important to stress that a measurement on an occasional basis, e. g., after the system release or after six months, is not sufficient. Only continuous measurement and control ensure the constant quality of the results the application delivers and, thereby, ensure customer satisfaction. Tendencies such as changing access rates, quality of system response, or changes in the types of questions users ask are observable. The early recognition of these tendencies and a quick reaction guarantee the fulfillment of the overall objectives and the long-term payback of the application.

The measurement of success can be based on various sources, correlated or used for dynamic trend analysis:

- quantitative data on the use of the application (access frequency, ratio of successfully answered requests, unsolved requests, the 10 most often asked questions, and so on),
- qualitative statements from user feedback (satisfaction, access frequency, and so on),
- quantitative data from connected systems (e.g. in the case of a call-tracking system: number of calls, number of call backs, duration of calls; in the case of a diagnosis of complex equipment: number of failures, time required to diagnose failures, percentage of "No Fault Founds" responses).

This data can be related to the forecasted volume of customer requests and the respective cost without the CBR system. The objectives of the measurement and control process are two:

1. to justify the investments and the spent efforts against the management and thereby indirectly influence the pricing of your company's services and products,
2. to provide guides for the optimization of the system, similar to an analysis of weak points.

**Rule of Thumb:** Define measures of success and establish control processes that enable continuous measurement of success and continuous improvement.

## 4.7 Direct Access for the Customer

*Reduce your costs by offering self-service.*

An important advantage of capturing knowledge and experience with a CBR system is the opportunity to provide the customer with direct access to corporate know-how. Even if this were not a priority in the first place, when planning the CBR application, you should make it a mid-term goal.

The strategy behind such an approach is call *avoidance*. Enable your customers to get the information they require directly from your homepage on the Internet and you will empower them to solve minor or routine problems themselves. CBR offers access to your knowledge via the Internet or on CD-ROM with three definite advantages:

1. *Reduce your cost of customer support*: A successful strategy of call avoidance reduces the cost of personnel at the call center and the support department. Employees become more productive and can focus their attention on the important tasks, since the amount of routine requests will be reduced significantly. This also increases the employees' satisfaction and thereby reduces the fluctuation of personnel at the call center.

2. *Worldwide 24/7 support*: Because of the high cost, it is impossible in most cases to operate a call center 24 hours, 7 days a week. Additionally, the global competition results in a clientele from different countries or even continents. A centralized call center would be overstrained by the diversity of languages and the different time zones. A CBR-based self-service solution empowers the customer to permanently access sales and service information from any point in the world, while in the meantime, helping your company avoid the costs and problems of a centralized all-time call center.

3. *Surplus value for the customer*: The continuous change of the business processes towards more and more self-service also reduces the customer's overhead expenses. Additionally, the consumed service is perceived as being of higher value by the customer since he or she determines and controls it.

Based on our experiences in building CBR applications we recommend that each company plans a direct access for its customers at the beginning of the CBR project. The reasons are twofold: First, we observe an increasing tendency towards self-service solutions and a strong acceptance of such offers; second, such access has an influence on the structure and design of the case base, as well as on the design of user interfaces. In general, state-of-the-art CBR tools allow for the easy modification of the user interfaces without requiring a change in the underlying domain model and case base. If the belated introduction of the direct access for customers requires structural changes to the model and cases, a complete redesign of the application may result.

However, in many cases it makes sense to open access for the customers later. The system should be in use internally in the company until the contents and results are sufficiently correct and completely cover the application domain. Never abuse the customer as a beta-tester of your services.

**Rule of Thumb:** Reduce your service costs and offer an actual surplus value for your customers by providing direct access to your CBR applications. The benefits outweigh the risks of disclosing parts of your know-how.

## 4.8 Market Your Success

*Do not forget to advertise the use of your CBR system.*

The introduction of a CBR system will have the desired results only if the system and the contained knowledge are intensely exploited. Only then will the investments be paid back, weak points of the application be discovered and relevant optimizations take place.

In many cases incentives have proven to be the right means to stimulate employees to use the new CBR system during the introductory. Incentives and competition are important internal marketing tools to boost the exploitation of the system. These can be combined with a commendation or bonus for employees who contribute to the system's improvement or who add significantly to establishing the best practice in knowledge management within the company.

The use of self-service solutions by customers must be advertised, too, e.g. note the URL of your Internet service pages on manuals, online-help texts, and so on. Even the phone message at the queue of the call center can be used to raise the awareness of self-service offers. Customers who deliver valuable feedback should be taken seriously and be thanked explicitly or even given a gift. The aim of such measures is to support the call-avoidance strategy, as well as to intensify the customer relationship.

Venturing into knowledge management, and thereby strategically improving service and support, is a strong marketing argument in itself for the affected products and the whole company. In the end, the surplus value for the prospect or customer is decisive, e.g. service around the clock, reduced cost of service, improved quality of service, and so on.

Investments in CBR systems pay back, if those who benefit from the application are aware of its advantages and how they have benefited. Therefore, marketing and advertising to disseminate these advantages are necessary.

**Rule of Thumb:** The ROI of a CBR system depends upon its regular use. Stimulate it by promoting it with marketing.

## 4.9  Expand the Scope

*Expand the scope of your CBR application.*

The general objective of almost every knowledge-management project is to disseminate and propagate the use of the best practices throughout an organization. Even if this started in a particular department, you should spread a successful application over the whole company and maybe beyond.

We recommend you to start with a clear-cut application area. Anyway, you should always keep in mind the possibility of extending the coverage of the CBR application itself, as well as a wider deployment of the system. Look out for such opportunities. A case base may contain knowledge of the company, products, processes, problem solutions, technologies, and so forth. If the mission of the CBR system was to improve customer support it was to be used mainly by service employees and customers then there would be no reason to keep this restriction for all time. Other company departments such as marketing or research and development, might benefit from the application, too. The same holds for business partners, e.g., suppliers as well as retail and sales organizations.

It is also possible to use external sources to keep the system up to date and to maintain it. Suppliers and sales organizations can provide valuable experience and know-how that should be integrated into the CBR application.

By including business partners and diverse company departments into the use and the maintenance of the CBR system, new synergistic effects can be obtained. This may go as far as making a real business out of the application itself.

"Start small and grow fast!" is a well-known maxim. It directly applies to the deployment of CBR systems. Start with a clear-cut area of application and a small group of users, but expand both whenever there is the chance to do so. There exist diverse possibilities and directions:

- extending the scope of the knowledge base,
- extending the area of application,
- providing access for more company departments,
- co-operating with business partners,
- establishing the CBR application as a profit-center,
- Licensing the system to other companies.

The investment in CBR systems and applications is a strategic decision. Setting up the first case base can be viewed as the first step towards full corporate knowledge management. It is a challenging and continuous process that offers lots of opportunities: optimized customer support, cost reductions, improved business practices, take up and dissemination of best practices, unique selling points, and new sources of revenue, to name a few.

**Rule of Thumb:** Transfer successful CBR applications to other products and company divisions in a long-term plan to include your business partners in it and actually make it a source of revenue.

# 5. Professional Case-Based Reasoning Application Development

Today, contemporary IT companies are facing a market that demands large-scale CBR projects and CBR software that fulfills quality standards. Therefore, a systematic and professional methodology for developing CBR applications is mandatory.

This chapter presents such a systematic approach. It is particularly suited for IT companies that develop professional CBR applications on a regular basis. In such cases, significant CBR experience accumulates and must be preserved as corporate knowledge. This chapter shows in detail a systematic procedure for capturing and representing CBR application development experience, based on recent software engineering methodologies and in line with current quality standards. Therefore, Chapter 6 shows how to represent CBR application development experience using software process models.

# 5.1  Why Do You Need the INRECA Methodology?

### 5.1.1  How You Benefit from a Methodology

A *methodology* combines a number of methods into a philosophy that addresses a number of phases of the software development life cycle (Booch, 1994). The methodology gives the guidelines for the activities that need to be performed in order to successfully develop a certain kind of software, in our case, a CBR application. These guidelines must be expressed in a well-defined terminology that enables the exchange of software development experience to continuously improve the development process.

Using an appropriate methodology should provide significant, quantifiable benefits in terms of

– *productivity*, e.g., reducing the risk of wasted efforts,
– *quality*, e.g., including quality deliverables,
– *communication*, i.e., formal and informal communication among members of the development team, and
– *management decision making,* e.g., planning, resource allocation, and monitoring (Bergmann et al. 1997).

One of the main driving forces behind the development and use of a methodology is the need for quality in both the products and processes during development of computer-based systems. This general observation holds for software development in general and for CBR application development in particular. Some methodologies and approaches to software development in general already exist, but software engineering methodology is still a major issue in current Software Engineering (SE) research. By adapting techniques originating in this area, we present a methodology based on recent SE techniques, which have been enriched by the experience of building and maintaining CBR applications.

### 5.1.2  What the INRECA Methodology Can Do for You

When building a CBR application for daily use in an existing client organization, the system developer must consider a large variety of different kinds of processes. To reach the goals described above, a methodology must cover the following aspects, which occur naturally, more or less, in every software-development project:

- the process of *project management* (cost and resource assessment, time schedules, project plans, quality control procedures, and so on),
- the specification of the different kinds of *products* or *deliverables* (including software deliverables) that must be produced,
- the process of *(technical) product development* and *maintenance*, which contains all technical tasks that are involved in the development and maintenance of the software,
- the *analysis* and, if necessary, the *(re-)organization* of the environment (e.g., a department) in which the CBR system will be introduced.

All these processes have to be defined and tailored according to the needs and circumstances of the current client. This activity requires a lot of practical experience. Although this experience is available in the minds of experienced application developers, it is usually not collected and stored systematically. This creates serious problems, e.g., when employees depart or when companies grow and new staff must be trained. But there is also an additional reason for documenting the software-development process: ensuring the quality of the produced software.

### 5.1.3  Ensuring High-Quality Software

A very important issue in general business life today is the demand that products fulfill certain quality standards. Customers are more fastidious with industrial products. Producing companies have to prove that the production of their deliverables follows processes that can guarantee certain degrees of quality. The most important international standards for so-called quality assurance systems are Iso 9000 and SPICE. Although they do not guarantee the quality of a product, they contain guidelines for developing a management system for quality assurance. The INRECA methodology supports recent quality standards. The documentation that is produced by following the INRECA methodology guarantees that the development process of the CBR applications can be traced.

## 5.2  Foundations from Software Engineering

The INRECA methodology has its origin in recent software engineering research and practices. It makes use of a software engineering paradigm that enables the reuse of software development experience by an organizational structure called *experience factory* (Basili et al., 1994). An *experience factory* is an organizational unit within a software development company or department that supports capturing and reusing software development experience and thereby supports project planning. It links with project execution so that lessons learned from previous projects can be reused. In the INRECA methodology, the experience factory provides the organizational framework for storing, accessing, and extending the guidelines for CBR application development, which are the core assets of the methodology.

The guidelines themselves are documented in a process-oriented view. *Software process modeling* (Rombach & Verlage, 1995) is a well-established area in software engineering that provides fundamentals for this. Software process models describe the flow of activities and the exchanged results during software application development.

In a nutshell, the INRECA methodology consists of collected CBR development experiences, represented as software process models and stored in the experience base of an experience factory. The experience factory itself provides the organizational structure to access this experience and to keep it alive and up-to-date. We now describe the experience factory paradigm and the basics of software process modeling in more detail.

### 5.2.1  The Experience Factory and the Quality Improvement Paradigm

The experience factory approach (Basili, et al. 1994) is motivated by the observation that any successful business requires a combination of technical and managerial solutions: a well-defined set of product needs to satisfy the customer, assist the developer in accomplishing those needs, and create competencies for future business; a well-defined set of processes to accomplish what needs to be accomplished, to control development, and to improve overall business; and a closed-loop process that supports learning and feedback.

An experience factory is a logical and/or physical organization that supports project development by analyzing and synthesizing all kinds of experience, acting as a repository for such experience, and supplying that experience to various projects on demand. An experience factory packages experience and collects it in an *experience base*. The experience consists of informal or formal models and measures of various software processes, products, and other forms of knowledge. Figure. 5.1 shows a schematized description of the experience factory, its steps, and its relation to the project organization. The project organization is in charge of *planning* and performing (*plan execution*) the software development project in an IT company. The experience factory *analyzes* the lessons learned from executed projects and records them in the experience base. To enable best reuse, these experiences are further *packaged*, i.e., they are generalized, tailored, and formalized. Further, the experience factory provides access to its experience base and thereby *supports* the project planning, which goes on in the project organization.

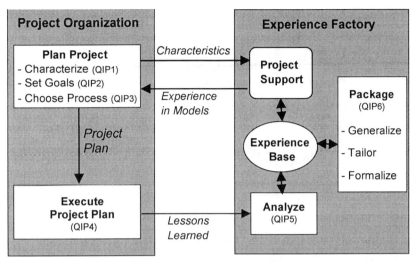

**Fig. 5.1.** The experience factory approach (adapted from Basili et al., 1994).

All these steps are organized into a cycle that enables the quality of the software development to be improved continuously. This cycle is called *the quality improvement paradigm* (QIP, see Fig. 5.2) and orders the six basic steps from the experience factory. In more detail, the six QIP steps are:

**Characterize (QIP1).** The aim of this step is to characterize the project and its environment based on the available information. Normally, a large variety of project characteristics and environmental factors can be used for this characterization, such as the application domain, susceptibility to changes, problem constraints, techniques, tools, programming language, existing software, available budget, the number of people, the level of their expertise, and so on. This step provides a context for goal definition and for selecting reusable experiences from the experience base.

**Set Goals (QIP2).** The goals of the project need to be defined. There are a variety of viewpoints for defining goals, like those viewpoints of the user, customer, project manager, corporation, and so on. Goals should be measurable, depending on the business models.

**Choose Process (QIP3).** On the basis of the characterization, the goals, and the previous experience from the experience base, appropriate processes for implementing the project must be chosen. This results in the overall project plan.

**Execute (QIP4).** The project plan is enacted, causing the development project to be carried out. For further analysis, respective records of the development process must be made.

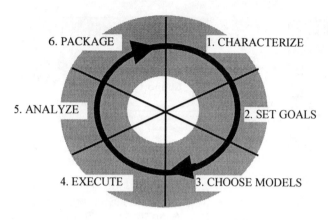

**Fig. 5.2.** The quality improvement paradigm (QIP).

**Analyze (QIP5).** At the end of each specific project, the data collected must be analyzed to evaluate current practices. Valuable, reusable experience must be identified.

**Package (QIP6).** The experience in the experience base consists of a variety of models. These models have to be defined and refined. Such models can be, e.g., resource models, process definitions and models, quality models, lessons learned, and so on. On the basis of the new experience, these models might get generalized, tailored to a particular kind of situation, or formalized, so that they can be reused in other projects.

The experience factory/quality improvement paradigm is especially tailored for the software business. It can be compared to approaches used in other fields of businesses, e.g., Total Quality Management. The experience factory and the quality improvement paradigm, provide a mechanism for continuous improvement through the experimentation, packaging, and reuse of experiences based on the needs of a business.

### 5.2.2 Software Process Modeling

Within the INRECA methodology, software process modeling (Rombach and Verlage 1995) is the means for documenting CBR experience. It provides a well-defined terminology. Software process models describe the engineering of a product, e.g., the software that has to be produced. Several documentation formalisms and several terminologies for process models have already been developed (Dellen et al. 1997). Although the particular names that are used in the different representation languages vary from one representation to another, all representations have a notation of *processes, methods,* and *products.*[1] Figure. 5.3 shows a graphical representation of these main elements.

**Processes.** A process is a basic step that has to be carried out in a software development project. It is an activity that has the goal of transforming some *input product*(s) into some *output product*(s). To enact a process, different alternative *methods* may be available that allow the required output products to be created in a systematic way, a process is typically defined by the following properties:

— A particular *goal* of such a basic step. The goal specifies *what* has to be achieved.
— A set of different alternative *methods* that can be used to implement the step. Such a method specifies one particular way of carrying out the process, i.e., one way of reaching the process's goal.
— *Input, output,* and *modified products* that describe which products are required at the beginning of the step, which products must be delivered at the end, and which products are changed during enactment.
— A set of *resources* (agents or tools) that are required to perform the step. Here the necessary qualifications or specifications that an agent or a tool must have so that (s)he/it can be assigned to the process are defined.

**Methods.** Methods contain a detailed specification of a particular way of reaching the goal of a process. A method can be either *simple* or *complex.* While a simple method provides only a description of what to do to reach the goal of the associated process, a complex method specifies a set of subprocesses, a set of intermediate products (called *byproducts*), and the flow of products among the subprocesses. This allows the definition of very flexible process models in a hierarchical manner, because very different process refinements can be described by using alternative subprocess models.

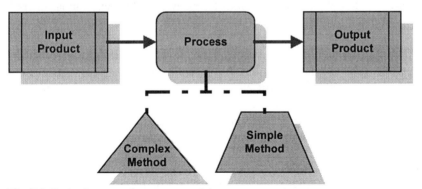

**Fig. 5.3.** Basic elements of a process model.

---

[1] Processes are also called *tasks* and products are called *deliverables.*

**Product.** The main goal of processes is to create or modify products. Products include the executable software system, as well as the documentation, like design documents or user manuals.

**Resources.** *Resources* are entities necessary to perform the tasks. Resources can be either *agents* or *tools*. Agents are models for humans or teams (e.g., managers, domain experts, designers, or programmers) that can be designated to perform a processes. The most relevant properties of agents are their qualifications. Tools (e.g., a modeling tool, a CBR tool, or a GUI builder) are used to support the enactment of a process and can be described by a specification. Therefore, by using the required qualifications and specifications defined in the generic process, it is possible to determine available agents and tools that can be assigned to a certain process.

## 5.3. The CBR Experience Base

The basic philosophy behind the INRECA methodology is the experience-based construction of CBR applications. The approach is particularly suited because CBR application development is an activity that relies heavily on experience. In certain areas, application development is already a routine task with clearly identified processes. This holds, for example, in the area of simple electronic product catalogs or simple help-desk applications. However, in recent years, CBR has entered new, important application areas that require large-scale application development. During the course of INRECA, three major application areas have been explored and large-scale industrial applications developed. The experiences of these developments have been captured and are the core of the INRECA methodology. Part III of this book and the attached CD-ROM present this experience in detail. We expect the market for many new CBR applications to open up in the future. Therefore, the involved IT companies need to build up their own area-specific experience. To explore such new fields systematically, the experience must be captured, represented, and accumulated for reuse. The experience factory idea in the INRECA methodology is perfectly suited for this purpose. A second big advantage in the context of a CBR methodology is that the basic idea behind the experience factory is closely related to the general idea of CBR, i.e., retrieving, reusing, revising, and retaining experience (Althoff et al. 1998; Althoff and Wilke 1997). The experience factory stores specific experience, namely software engineering experience, in a case base, which we call an *experience base*. Thus, the motivation and rationale behind the experience factory approach should be easily understandable by people who are familiar with the Case-Based Reasoning approach in general.

### 5.3.1 Experience Captured in Software Process Models

In the INRECA methodology, software process models represent the CBR development experience that is stored in the experience base. Such software processes can be very abstract, i.e., they can represent some very coarse development steps such as domain model definition, similarity measure definition, and case acquisition. Or they can be very detailed and specific for a particular project, such as analyzing data from Analog Device Inc. operational amplifier (OpAmp) product database, selecting relevant OpAmp specification parameters, and so on. The software process modeling approach allows the construction of such a hierarchically organized set of process models. Abstract processes can be described by complex methods, which are themselves a set of more detailed processes. We make use of this property to structure the experience base.

### 5.3.2 Experience on Different Levels of Abstraction

The experience base is organized on three levels of abstraction: a *common generic level* at the top, a *cookbook level* in the middle, and a *specific project level* at the bottom (Bergmann et al. 1998). These levels are shown in Fig. 5.4.

**Common Generic Level.** At this level, processes, products, and methods are collected that are common for a very large spectrum of different CBR applications. The documented processes usually appear during the development of most CBR applications. The documented methods are very general and widely applicable, and give general guidance for how the respective processes can be enacted. At this common level, processes are not necessarily connected to a complete product flow that describes the development of a complete CBR application. They can be

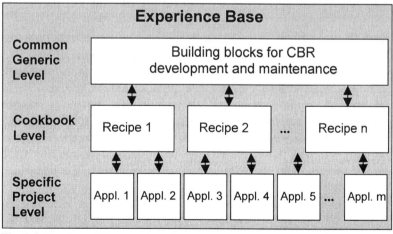

**Fig. 5.4.** Structure of the experience base.

isolated entities that can be combined in the context of a particular application or application class. Chapter 4 presented CBR development experience on such a common generic level. For a more detailed version, please consult the INRECA CD-ROM.

**Cookbook level.** At this level, processes, products, and methods are tailored for a particular class of applications (e.g., help desk, technical maintenance, product catalogue). For each application class, the cookbook level contains a so-called *recipe*. Such a recipe describes how an application of that kind should be developed and/or maintained. Thus process models contained in such a recipe provide specific guidance for the development of a CBR application of this application class. Usually, these items are more concrete versions of items described at the common generic level. Unlike processes at the common generic level, all processes that are relevant for an application class are connected and build a product flow from which a specific project plan can be developed. Chapters 7, 8, and 9 describe three recipes from the cookbook level.

**Specific project level.** The specific project level describes experience in the context of a single, particular project that has already been carried out. It contains project-specific information, such as the particular processes that were carried out, the effort that was required for these processes, the products that were produced, the methods that were used to perform the processes, and the people who were involved in executing the processes. It is a complete documentation of the project, which is more and more important today to guarantee the quality standards (e.g., ISO 9000 or SPICE) required by industrial clients. For examples of applications documented on the specific project level, please consult the INRECA CD-ROM.

## 5.4 How to Apply the INRECA Methodology to New Projects

When a new CBR project is being planned, the relevant experience from the experience base must be selected and reused. This relates to the steps QIP1 to QIP3 of the quality improvement paradigm (see Fig. 5.2). The recipes at the cookbook level are particularly useful for building a new application that directly falls into one of the covered application classes. The recipes are the most valuable knowledge captured in the methodology. Therefore, one should first investigate the cookbook-level to identify whether a cookbook recipe can be reused directly. If this is the case, the new CBR project can be considered a standard CBR application, and the processes from the respective recipe can provide immediate guidance for setting up the new project. On the other hand, if the new project does not fall into one of the application classes covered by the recipe, then the new project enters a new application area. In that case, the new project plan must be constructed from scratch. However, the processes described in the common generic level can be used to assemble the new project plan. Figure 5.5, shows the overall procedure for applying the INRECA methodology. It is a special variant of steps 1-4 of the quality improvement paradigm.

1. **Characterize New CBR Project:** Identify the application area of the new CBR project. The goal is to decide whether an existing recipe from the cookbook level of the methodology covers this application.

2. **Recipe Available:** Identify whether an appropriate recipe is available. If this is the case then continue with step 3a; otherwise continue with step 4a.

3a. **Analyze Processes from Recipe**: An appropriate recipe is available. The process model contained in this recipe must now be analyzed to see whether it can be mapped and tailored to the application at hand.

3b. **Select Similar Specific Project:** Analyze the project descriptions on the specific project level. If a similar project is available then it should be identified as to whether some of the specific experience can be reused

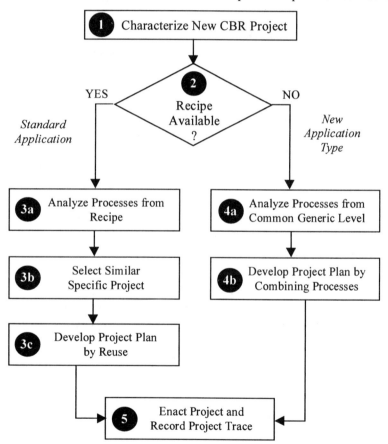

**Fig. 5.5.** How to use the experience base.

within the scope of the current project. This might be a specific way to implement a certain process or software component. It can help to identify existing software components from previous projects that can be reused immediately on the code level.

**3c.**  **Develop New Project Plan by Reuse.** Develop a project plan for the new project. This project plan is based mainly on a process model from the selected experience recipe. However, application-specific tailoring and pragmatic modifications are typically required. If components from similar projects can be identified for reuse, the project plan must take care of this fact to avoid re-development efforts.

**4a.**  **Analyze Processes from Common Generic Level.** The set of processes described at the common generic level should be analyzed in the context of the new project. The goal is to identify those processes that are important for the new application. These processes can be considered the building blocks from which the new project plan can be assembled.

**4b.**  **Develop Project Plan by Combining Processes.** Based on the selected processes, a new project plan must be assembled. For this purpose, the processes must be made more precise and operational. Depending on how innovative the new application area is, it might even be necessary to develop new methods or software components.

**5.**  **Enact Project and Record Project Trace.** Execute the project by enacting the project plan. Document the experience during the enactment of this project. Particularly, note all deviations from the developed project plan. This is important for two reasons. First, to ensure that the development is performed according to the necessary quality standards and, second, to feedback the new experience into the experience base for reuse.

## 5.5 Capturing Your Own CBR Experience

After a project is finished, it is very important that the experience and the lessons learned are not lost, but are captured for inclusion into the experience base, which is the core of the INRECA methodology. This is necessary for continuous improvement of the CBR software-development process. This maintenance activity is related to steps 5 and 6 of the quality improvement paradigm (see Fig. 5.2). For the INRECA methodology, a particular extension and update procedure for the experience base has been developed (see Fig. 5.6).

**6.**  **Analyze Project Trace.** Collect all information that had been captured about the finished project. Analyze this information and identify the processes that were actually performed during the enactment of the project.

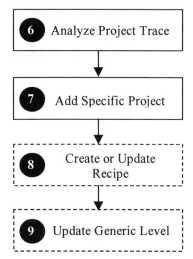

**Fig. 5.6.** Adding new experience.

**7.  Add Specific Project.** Document the project by creating a specific process description that accurately describes what has been done in the project. Add this process description to the specific project level of the INRECA experience base. If appropriate, create links to the cookbook-level recipes from which this project had been derived.

**8.  Create or Update Recipe (optional).** Based on the experience collected from the new project, it might become necessary to update an existing recipe or even to create a completely new one. An existing recipe might need to be updated if the following situation was encountered: A recipe was used to setup the project plan for the current project (step 3a in Fig. 5.5) but the experience from enacting the project indicated significant deviations from this plan. In this case, an update of the recipe is required to cover this newly learned lessons.

A new recipe might need to be created, if CBR was applied to a new type of application that was not covered by any of the existing recipes (steps 4a+b in Fig. 5.5). The process description for the new specific project can then be generalized into a new cookbook-level recipe. For this purpose, all project-specific information must be abstracted so that only those pieces remain that are likely to be reused for new, similar applications. It is very likely that this generalization process can be achieved only after several projects of this new application area have been realized. This avoids generalizing single experiences and is more reliable.

9.    **Update Generic Level (optional).** If during the previous steps some new generic processes, methods, or products can be identified that are of more general interest, i.e., relevant for more than one application class, then they should be added to the common generic level of the experience base.

## 5.6  The INRECA Methodology and Quality Standards

Previously, we noted the increasing importance of quality assurance systems and how they provide the reader with information concerning the requirements of these standards. CBR applications based on the INRECA methodology fulfill these requirements. That means that a company developing such software products can easily get the audit for their product.

The major advantage of developing a CBR application following the INRECA methodology is the systematic documentation in a predefined format of every process. Tools exist that support the documentation in a user-friendly way. See chapter 6 and the INRECA CD-ROM for details.

# 6. Documenting Case-Based Reasoning Development Experience

In this chapter, the basic concepts and, in particular, the terminology of software process modeling are introduced at a level of detail that is sufficient for potential users of the INRECA methodology. The basic terms that were first mentioned in the previous chapter are now explained more precisely. Additionally, the INRECA methodology tool that supports the documentation of the CBR development experience is introduced.

## 6.1  Into the Details of Processes, Products, and Methods

### 6.1.1  Software Processes: The Basic Activities

A *process* is a basic step - an activity -  in a software development project. Each process has a particular *goal* that it must achieve. Typically, a process is named for this goal. Examples are: "Analysis of system requirements," "Development of a system design," and "Implementation of the software components." These are examples of high-level technical processes that usually occur in every software project.

A process usually has a set of defined input, output, and modified products. For example, one input of a software implementation process is some kind of design document and the output is usually the produced code and the documentation of that code. A process always transforms the given input into a desired output. A modified product is basically a product that is both an input and output product at the same time. In the following, we use the term *product* for everything that occurs as the input or output of a process, or gets modified by a process. A software design document is an example of a product. Another example is a piece of software that is produced. The final system being delivered is usually the main output product of the technical software development processes.

To enact a process in a systematic way, different alternative *methods* are applicable. A given method specifies one particular way of carrying out the process, i.e., one means of creating the output products of the process. When planning a project, you must select the method that is most appropriate for implementing the process in the particular context of the current project. For example, a method for implementing a graphical user interface may be to code it solely in C using only the X-Windows primitives. Another method is to use a GUI-builder to design the interface and to link events to graphical elements. A third method is to reuse and adapt the code of an existing, very similar user interface.

The enactment of a process involves several *resources*. These can be human resources, called *agents*, who are actively enacting the processes and who are responsible for delivering the output product(s) of the process. Software *tools* are resources that are used by an agent during enactment of the process. For example, a programmer is an agent who is actively involved in the process of implementing a software module. S/he uses a GUI-builder to produce the GUI software and a word processor to write the GUI documentation. Both, the GUI-builder and the word processor are resources in the form of tools.

### 6.1.2 Technical, Organizational, and Managerial Processes

We distinguish three types of processes that are involved in a software development project:

- technical processes,
- organizational processes,
- managerial processes.

**Technical Processes.** First of all, there are the *technical processes,* which describe the development of the system and the required documentation itself. Some of the technical processes that are part of most software development projects are, for instance, requirements analysis, system design, implementation, and testing.

**Organizational Processes.** The second kind of processes that are part of most standard software development processes are the *organizational processes.* They address those parts of the user organization's business process in which the software system will be embedded. New processes have to be introduced into an existing business process, such as training end-users or the technical maintenance of the system. Existing processes may need to be changed or re-organized to make the best use of the new software system. For example, the introduction of a help-desk system for hot-line support, requires new processes for training the hot-line personnel, for archiving request-records, and for updating and maintaining the help-desk system.

**Managerial Processes.** The third kind of processes are *managerial processes.* The primary goal of managerial processes is to provide an environment and services for the development of software that meet the product requirements and project goals, i.e., services for enacting the technical and the organizational processes. Examples of managerial processes are project planning, monitoring, and quality assurance. The following boxed paragraph summarizes the three kinds of process types:

In a software development project, several processes of these types typically interact. The next section will examine this assertion.

### 6.1.3 How Processes Interact

Typically, a process produces an output product that is used as an input to another process. For example, the process "Perform Feasibility Study" produces as its main output an "Evaluation Document" product. Then, this evaluation document is used as input for the process "Perform First Project Phase." Figure 6.1 shows this kind of interaction between these two processes. This figure also shows the graphical notation the INRECA methodology uses for processes and products. For processes, we use rectangles with rounded edges, while products are displayed as rectangles with a double line on the left and right side. Processes and products are connected by different kinds of arrows. An arrow from a process to a product denotes that the product is contained in the output-products description of the process, i.e., it is produced by the process. An arrow from a product to a process denotes that the product is contained in the input-products description of the process, i.e., it is required by the process. A double-headed arrow between a product and a process denotes that the product is contained in the modified-products description of the process, i.e., it is modified by the process (no double-headed arrows occur in Fig. 6.1).

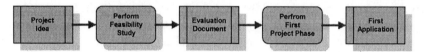

**Fig. 6.1.** Interaction among processes.

For each process, there can be several alternative methods that describe alternatives to enacting the process. Simple methods are graphically denoted by a trapezoid, while complex methods are printed as a triangle. Figure 6.2 shows the "Feasibility Study" process together with two alternative complex methods.

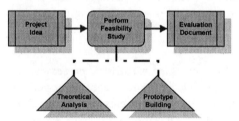

**Fig. 6.2.** Two alternative complex methods.

Complex methods are called complex because they consist of several subprocesses connected in a particular way. Together, these subprocesses describe the details of how to enact the respective complex method. For example the method "Prototype Building" can be described in further detail by the subprocesses and the product flow shown in Fig 6.3. All these subprocesses have to be enacted in order to implement the complex method "Prototype Building." Please note that as a result of the subprocesses of a method, all required output products of the higher-level process must be produced. In the example shown here, the "Evaluation Document" is created by the product flow shown in Fig. 6.3 and is further used in Fig 6.1 as input to the process "Perform First Project Phase."

By this approach, the whole software development activity can be divided into several isolated parts that are easy to understand. Also, these parts can be reused individually for new projects or modules.

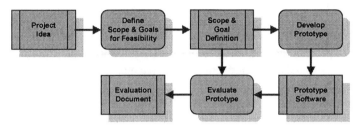

**Fig. 6.3.** Product flow for the complex method "Prototype Building".

### 6.1.4 Combining Processes to Process Models

One of the main ideas behind software process modeling is to make explicit all the processes, products, methods, resources, and interactions of which a software project consists. These are kinds of information that contain very valuable experience about the software development process. They should be captured, stored, and reused for setting up and implementing new projects. The processes, products, and methods must be identified and documented in a clear and understandable way. The diagrams alone are not sufficient for this purpose. Each of the elements that occur in a diagram must be described in sufficient detail. Sections 6.2 and 6.3 show in detail how processes, products, and methods are documented in the INRECA methodology. Such a description of processes, products, and methods is called a *process model*. Obviously, making these elements explicit provides a solid basis for project planning. For example, the effort required for the project can be calculated based on the processes involved in the project. Explicitly documented processes and the management of the products that arise also support the execution and monitoring of a project. Documenting processes is also essential for controlling and improving the quality of the product (software) being produced. Documentation is also essential to ensure compliance with current quality standards.

## 6.2  Generic and Specific Descriptions

The INRECA methodology distinguishes between *generic* and *specific* descriptions for processes, products, and methods. The differences will be made clear in the following sections.

### 6.2.1 Generic Descriptions

The *generic descriptions* describe processes, products, and methods in a way that is independent of a specific development project. They contain generalized information that is likely to be useful in several specific situations.

Again consider, for instance, the process of building a GUI for a CBR application. The process "GUI Development" has one input product, namely the document describing the specification of the GUI, and two output products, one for the software implementing the GUI and one for the documentation describing how to use the GUI. The generic description of the input product (GUI specification document) declares what information in general should be contained in a GUI specification document. It does not say anything about a particular GUI to be developed within a project. Moreover, the generic description of the GUI building process should also specify that one agent is required who has programming capabilities and who is familiar with a GUI-builder, and that a tool is required, namely a GUI-builder, that is flexible enough to produce the kind of GUI that is required. All this is generic information, not restricted to a single project and, therefore widely applicable. The generic description does not contain any information on exactly what the GUI looks like, which person is actually allocated to the task of building the GUI, or which particular GUI-builder is used. The generic information only describes requirements of agents or tools, and general guidelines on how to execute a process.

Generic descriptions are the most important part of the experience base. They are used to document the common generic level and the cookbook level of our experience base (see section 5.3).

### 6.2.2     Specific Descriptions

*Specific descriptions* elaborate processes, products, and methods for a particular development project. Usually, they are created after the project is finished. Specific descriptions contain information such as the specific agents who were involved in enacting the process and specific tools that were used. For the purpose of documentation, they can also contain information about the effort that was spent for a process, and so forth.

Consider, for instance, a specific GUI development process as it occurs in a project, let's say, in the Analog Devices Application described in section 3.2. The specific description for this process contains information about the input and output products, e.g., the Analog Devices GUI specification, Analog Devices GUI software, and Analog Devices GUI documentation. It contains references to the specific Analog Devices GUI specification document from the project. Moreover, it also contains information about the particular programmer who built the GUI (e.g., James Simon) and about the particular GUI-builder tool that was used (e.g., Visual Basic).

## 6.3 Detailed Description of Process Models

Generic and specific processes, products, and methods are documented (and stored in the experience base) using different types of sheets. One such sheet is like a structured page containing all relevant information about the respective item in a predefined format. The sheets help to standardize the documentation of the experience. They are created as Web pages, which can be viewed using a standard Internet browser. Hence, accessing the experience base becomes a very easy task that does not require any specialized knowledge. Altogcthcr, the following types of sheets are available:

— generic process description sheet,
— generic product description sheet,
— generic simple method description sheet,
— generic complex method description sheet,
— specific process description sheet,
— specific product description sheet,
— specific simple method description sheet,
— specific complex method description sheet.

Each sheet is a form that contains several predefined slots that should be filled in to document the process, product, or method. Before introducing these sheets in detail, we will give a brief overview of the different kinds of sheets and how they are related (see Figure 6.4). A single sheet is used to describe processes. This sheet will contain references to the respective input, output, and modified products of the process. Every product is documented by using a separate description sheet. The process description also contains references to the applicable methods. A method can be either a *simple method* (which is elementary and does not contain any

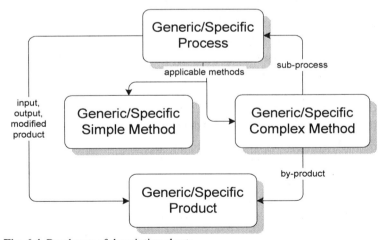

**Fig. 6.4.** Road map of description sheets.

references to other description sheets) or a *complex method*. A complex method connects several subprocesses (each of which is again documented as a separate generic process description), which may exchange some byproducts (documented as separate descriptions).

The sheets for the generic and specific items look very similar. They have the same fields for entering information. The difference is that in the specific sheets, the fields are filled with project-specific information, while in the generic sheets the fields contain project-independent, generalized information.

### 6.3.1  Process Description Sheets

Generic and specific *process description sheets* contain several fields to hold the information that is necessary for understanding what the process is supposed to do. Figure 6.5 shows an example of a generic process description sheet.

**Recipe/Project Name.** Every process belongs to a particular level in the experience base and within this level to a particular recipe or project. For generic description sheets, the name of the recipe is noted, for specific description sheets the name of the project is noted.

**Process Name.** The process name assigns each process description a unique identifier, i.e., a text string. The name should be as short as possible but should clearly identify the process. Names of generic process descriptions are subsequently used as references to the generic process description itself.

**Process Goal.** The goal describes *what* the process is supposed to do, specified by a textual description. The process goal does not state how the process is performed. This information is recorded in the methods. Obviously, the goal of a process is partially contained in the process name. Since the process name should be as short as possible, a more detailed goal specification is often required.

**Input Product, Output Product, Modified Product.** Input products are products that are required during the enactment of the process to achieve the desired result. Output products are products that are produced during the enactment of the process. Usually, the production of these output products is one of the goals of the process. Modified products are products that are changed or extended during the enactment of the process. Usually, the modification of these products is also one of the goals of the process. All products are referenced through the product name (see section 6.3.2). The respective product sheets can be reached by following the included HTML links.

**Applicable Method.** Applicable methods specify a set of alternative methods to implement the process. Typically, a process can be implemented by different methods from which one is selected to perform the process. A method describes *how* the goal of the process can be achieved. Here, we do not specify the contents

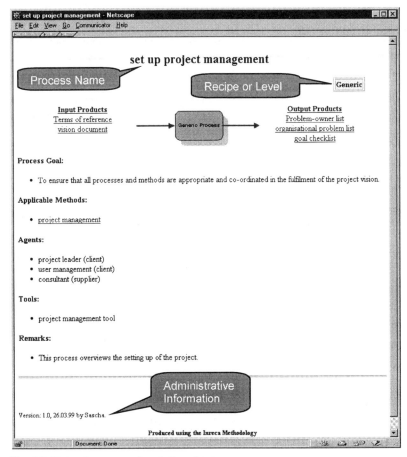

**Fig. 6.5.** Example process description sheet.

of the methods, but only the names of the methods. Each method should be described in a separate sheet that includes all required details (see sections 6.3.3 and 6.3.4). The respective method sheets can be reached by following the included HTML links.

**Agents.** Agents fields specify the type of agents (personnel) who are involved in the process, together with their qualifications and the kinds of the organizations to which they belong. The qualifications that the agent must have in order to execute the respective process is a very important issue. For instance, "experience in GUI development" is a proper qualification for a programmer involved in the GUI development process. One of the agents involved in the process has to be declared "responsible" for the process.

**Required Tools.** The required tool specification lists all kinds of tools that are required to enact the process. For each tool, the most important requirements should be noted as well. For instance "can import Word documents and export HTML" might be proper requirements for a word processor.

**Administrative Information.** Additionally, some administrative information about a sheet is required. This is important in order to maintain the sheets and to distinguish among different versions. This information is the name of the sheet author, the version of the sheet, and the date of the last change.

### 6.3.2  Product Description Sheets

Products may be software, text documents, graphics, sound, and so on. Generic and specific *product description sheets* contain several fields to hold the information that is necessary for understanding what the product consists of or should consist of. Figure 6.6 shows an example of a generic product description sheet.

**Module/Project Name.** This field mentions the recipe (for generic sheets) or the project (for specific sheets) to which the product belongs. This is the same as for the process description sheets.

**Product Name.** The name should be as short as possible but should clearly identify the product. Product names are used in the process description to specify the input, output, or modified product. Examples of appropriate product names are "Requirements Document" or "CBR Prototype Software."

**Product Description.** This is a detailed textual description of the product or a reference to a detailed "external" specification. From this description, it should become clear what product must be produced. If necessary, quality standards for the product also can be noted.

**Administrative Information.** The same administrative information is required as for the process description sheets.

### 6.3.3  Simple Method Description Sheets

Typically, there are several ways to enact a process. A *method* describes one such way. While the process declares WHAT should be done, a method explains HOW to do it. Simple methods describe the "How-To" using a short section of text. If a method needs to be described in more detail, complex method descriptions should be used (see section 6.3.4). Figure 6.7 shows an example of a generic simple-method description sheet. It consists of the following fields:

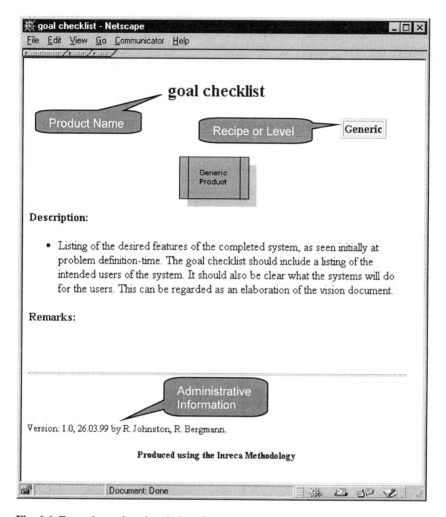

**Fig. 6.6.** Example product description sheet.

**Module/Project Name.** This field mentions the recipe (for generic sheets) or the project (for specific sheets) to which the product belongs. This is the same as for the process description sheets.

**Method Name.** The method name should be as short as possible but should clearly identify the method. Names of simple method descriptions are used in the applicable methods section of process descriptions (see section 6.3.1).

**Method Description.** The method description contains a "how-to" description about the enactment of the actual process. Such a description should contain all information necessary for the assigned agents to produce the specified products. Experiences from earlier projects can be captured in these descriptions by giving descriptions of "good" examples or warnings of steps that were not successful in the past. In general, this description will be informal, i.e., narrative text. However, if formalisms or schemata exist for structuring such descriptions, they should be used. For example, a simple method that describes the design of the similarity measure could give guidelines on how a local similarity measure should be chosen, depending on the kind of attributes.

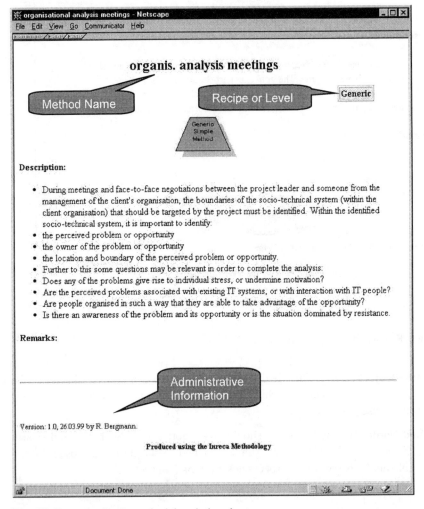

**Fig. 6.7.** Example simple method description sheet.

**Administrative Information.** The same administrative information is required as for the process description sheets.

### 6.3.4  Complex Method Description Sheets

Complex methods are necessary when a method needs to be described in more detail. In that case, a method itself can be decomposed into several subprocesses, which interact in a certain way and exchange products. Hence, a complex method consists of several subprocesses and the product flow among them. Figure 6.8 shows an example of a generic complex method description sheet. It consists of the following fields:

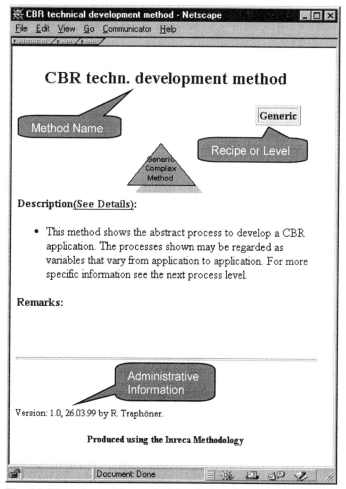

**Fig. 6.8.** Example complex method description sheet.

**Module/Project Name.** This field mentions the recipe (for generic sheets) or the project (for specific sheets) to which the product belongs. This is the same as for the process description sheets.

**Method Name.** Each complex method has a unique name. The method name should be as short as possible but should clearly identify the method. Names of complex method descriptions are used in the applicable methods section of process descriptions (see section 6.3.1).

**Method Description.** The method description contains a verbal description about the enactment of the actual process, similar to those of the simple methods. It should explain how the subprocesses shown in the "details section" (see below) should be enacted.

**Details.** The details section links to a product flow description for the complex method, like the one shown in Fig. 6.3. This contains the relevant subprocesses, and the created byproducts. Each of the subprocesses and byproducts has its own description on a separate sheet. Thereby, details can be added at several levels of abstraction, as appropriate, to describe the experience.

**Administrative Information.** The same administrative information is required as for the process description sheets.

## 6.4  Tool Support for Documenting the Experience

We can document a specific CBR project, a recipe for an application class, or common generic CBR development experience using the INRECA methodology tool. This tool describes projects in terms of a process diagram where each element of the diagram links to information about the process or product in a database. The tool supports the creation of a web site for a given project, allowing the documentation to be shared among distributed members of a development team. The INRECA methodology tool is implemented using the Visio modeling software from Visio Corporation. Visio is a graphical software tool that supports professionals in diagramming systems, structures, and processes in business environments. The basic element of a Visio document is the page. A collection of pages linked together in some sequence is a document. Individual pages generally contain shapes that are linked together on the page to create a drawing. Figures 6.1 to 6.3 give examples of such drawings created with the INRECA Methodology Tool.

Shapes, in turn, can be linked to other pages in the document. A given shape has a range of properties that can be edited using the Visio Professional Software Tool or using the developer's environment provided by Visual Basic for Applications. Visio provides a range of shape stencils, each of which contains the symbols for a specific kind of diagram or modeling approach. Some examples of the modeling approaches supported are Gane and Sarson DFD, Booch OOD, and SSADM.

### 6.4.1 Rationale for Selecting Visio

Reasons for selecting Visio to support the INRECA methodology are the following.

— Visio gives a good variety of standard shapes, which can be labeled, linked, and manipulated singly or in groups. Thus, we can have special shapes for products, processes, and methods.
— Shapes can be hot-linked to explanatory material to support the explanations of the meanings of the shapes and their linkages. We used this feature to attach the information contained in description sheets (see section 6.3) to the shapes.
— A recursive structure of Visio pages can be constructed, with an overview of the total project on page 1 and the shapes being hot-linked to subsequent Visio pages. Those pages develop the underlying detail, still in diagram form, and the shapes on these detail pages themselves can be hot-linked down to the underlying documentation.
— The Visio diagram can be saved in runtime mode as an HTML file with its hotlinks to other HTML files preserved, thus forming an integral part of a robust HTML system.
— Visio supports application development through an implementation of Visual Basic for Applications. This allows us to customize the Visio functionality to meet the needs of the INRECA methodology.
— Access to databases is supported by Visio, allowing us to maintain in a consistent database structure the documentation for a specific project or a recipe.

### 6.4.2 Standard Recursive Structure

The first page of the Visio diagram consists of a set of high-level process-shapes connecting input product shapes and output product shapes, possibly via one or more intermediate product-shapes. The page header has the project name (if specific), or the recipe name (if cookbook), or just states "Common Generic" for the top-level of the experience base (see section 5.3).

In general the processes can be linked to complex-method shapes, which are hot-linked to related Visio documents, each of which constitutes an overview explanation in diagram form of the complex method itself, and so on. The recursion stops when all processes in a diagram can be implemented using simple methods.

### 6.4.3  Managing Several Recipes and Projects

Typically, the CBR experience resides in an R&D group or a developmental IT department. Within this unit, the CBR experience base is likely to exist on one person's system, or on a local server accessible to a named group of experts. The directory structure supporting this experience base might consist of a root directory called "CBR Experience" that contains a set of Visio diagrams and associated explanatory sheets filled in at an abstract, generic level.

Within this directory there are also a set of subdirectories, each representing a domain of experience within which projects may be developed using a common set of cookbook experiences. Within each cookbook directory there are a set of project subdirectories, each containing the experience of a specific project.

The tool supports the creation of a plan for a specific project from a cookbook recipe. The resulting Visio document can then be used to allocate tasks in the project and to record the experience of the project team. This experience then can be used to revise the cookbook recipe, if necessary.

### 6.4.4  HTML Publication

Each project in the methodology can be easily published in HTML format. The tool will create the diagrams and sheets for the entire project, which can then be published on an Intranet or Internet site. The best practices of performing the development processes are maintained, and they become valuable means of sharing project knowledge and maintaining reference points.

The INRECA methodology tool and the Users Manual are on the INRECA CD-ROM attached to this book.

# Part III

# Using the Methodology in Different Domains

Part III, which consists of the chapter 7 through 9, shows, for three major application domains, how to develop CBR applications according to the INRECA methodology. Building on the foundations laid in part II of the book, lessons learned and reusable software process models are presented in detail.

**Chapter 7** "Developing Case-Based Help-Desk Support Systems for Complex Technical Equipment" describes the development process for CBR applications in the area of complex help-desks.

**Chapter 8** "Developing Intelligent Catalog Search Applications" explains how to develop sales support applications.

**Chapter 9** "Developing Maintenance Applications" focuses on the development process for maintenance of technical equipment.

In each of these chapters, the impact of applying the INRECA methodology is evaluated.

# 7. Developing Case-Based Help-Desk Support Systems for Complex Technical Equipment

Help-desks support end-users of complex technical equipment by providing guidance on the use of products and by performing maintenance operations when needed. Since the complexity and diversity of technical equipment increases continuously, help-desk operators have difficulty covering the entire range of relevant products and need a knowledge repository to be able to find the correct solution to a problem as soon as possible.

This chapter describes the processes that must be performed to develop a case-based system to support help-desk operators in diagnosing complex technical equipment. It is based on the help-desk recipe from the cookbook level in the INRECA methodology. The recipe was created during the development of the HOMER system described in section 3.1, and has been applied to the development of several other help-desk systems. Using the methodology, we were able to speed up the development process of a case-based help-desk support system by a factor of 12 (see section 7.5). Apart from the increase in productivity, the methodology also resulted in considerable benefits regarding product and process quality, provided a means of communication, and served as a basis for management decisions.

## 7.1  Characteristics of Case-Based Help-Desk Support Systems

The ever-increasing complexity of technical equipment makes it difficult for the users of these systems to operate and maintain them without support. While the probability that technical systems will fail grows exponentially with their complexity, the expertise needed to be able to control every feature of such complex systems usually exceeds the resources available to end-users.

Help-desks support end-users of complex technical equipment. When end-users have problems, they count on help-desks to provide emergency services. Help-desk operators provide guidance on how to use the system and keep the system operational by performing necessary maintenance tasks. They are expected to be able to solve problems on very short notice, in a very short time, and to be knowledgeable in all areas that are related to the technical system at hand.

Help-desk operators use their own experiences to solve most of the problems that are relayed to them. However, as systems become more complex, the areas help-desk operators are experts in tend to diverge, i.e., problem solving experience is distributed among experts and the areas of expertise do not necessarily overlap. Nevertheless, when an end-user has a problem, he or she wants it solved as soon as possible. If that expert is not available, the user has to wait, which is annoying and not acceptable in a commercial environment. The problem-solving experience must be available to every help-desk operator at all times.

Current trouble-ticket tools that are being used at help-desks do not provide a means of capturing and reusing problem-solving experience in a convenient and efficient manner. Since problem-solving experience is a corporate asset, it has to be collected, preserved, and used as efficiently and effectively as possible. The best way to achieve this is to use CBR  to develop help-desk support systems.

The goal of developing a case-based help-desk support system is to create a knowledge repository that contains problem-solving experiences for a complex technical domain that changes over time. This knowledge repository will be used in an organization, by a group of people with varying levels of expertise, in a time-critical operation. It is obvious that the development and use of such a system does not only involve technical processes, but also raises managerial and organizational issues. In the following sections, we describe the tasks that must be performed to develop a case-based help-desk support system and the processes that have to be put into place to make such a system operational.

**Tab. 7.1.** Processes during case-based help-desk support system development and use.

| | | System Development | System Use |
|---|---|---|---|
| **Managerial Processes** | | - Goal Definition<br>- Awareness Creation<br>- CBR-Tool Selection | - Progress Verification and Controlling |
| **Organizational Processes** | | - Project Team Selection<br>- Initial Domain Selection<br>- Project Team Training<br>- Knowledge Acquisition Process Development<br>- Utilization Process Development | - End-User Training<br>- Continuous Knowledge Acquisition<br>- Utilization Process |
| **Technical Processes** | **General IT-System Related** | - System Specification<br>- System Implementation<br>- System Integration<br>- System Verification | - Continuous System Maintenance |
| | **Knowledge Repository Related** | - Initial Knowledge Acquisition<br>- Core Knowledge Acquisition | - Continuous Knowledge Acquisition and Maintenance |

# 7.2 Development and Use of Case-Based Help-Desk Support Systems for Complex Technical Equipment

### 7.2.1 Process Types

Table 7.1 lists the processes that must be considered and performed during the development and use of a case-based help-desk support system. As described in section 6.1.2, we distinguish among managerial, organizational, and technical processes.

### 7.2.2 Managerial Processes During System Development

**Goal Definition.** For a case-based help-desk support system project to be successful, precise goals must be determined at the outset. This enables management to fix the direction in which the project should develop and to measure the success of the project upon completion. Hard (quantitative) and soft (qualitative) success criteria should be identified (cf. Stolpmann & Wess 1999). Hard criteria are measurable quantities and cover aspects like:

- *problem solution quality* (first-call resolution rate, solution correctness, and consistency, average cost of proposed solution, and so on),
- *process quality* (average time needed to solve a problem, average number of escalations needed, quality of dynamic priority assignment, and so on),
- *organizational quality* (speedup in help-desk operator training, flexibility of staffing, cost per interaction, and so on).

Soft criteria, on the other hand, measure the subjective quality of the help-desk and cover aspects like:

- *end-user satisfaction* (availability of the help-desk, perceived competence, friendliness, and so on),
- *help-desk operator satisfaction* (workload, work atmosphere, repetitiveness of tasks, intellectual stimulation, and so on), and
- *corporate aspects* (preservation of knowledge, publicity, and so on.).

The goals must be communicated to the project team, and the team has to be motivated to achieve them (see also chapter 4).

When project goals are selected, it is important that these goals be realistic both in terms of their time frame and whether they can be achieved with an acceptable amount of resources. The case-based help-desk support project must be seen as part of the long-term knowledge management strategy for the company. Since knowledge increases and evolves, the experience in a CBR system must be maintained continuously. System development is only the initial phase in any CBR project.

**Awareness Creation and Motivation.** The case-based help-desk support system project targets the most precious asset of the employees: their experience. The project's goal is to collect the problem-solving experience of each relevant employee and make it available to whomever needs it in the organization.

Obviously the help-desk operators will have a motivational barrier to giving away their experience. Every employee knows that "knowledge is power." In help-desk environments or domains where experience is being used to solve problems having experience translates into being superior and indispensable, whereas giving away the knowledge can be perceived as becoming obsolete.

However, as soon as help-desk operators become part of a project team and understand that sharing knowledge means that they will get back much more than they invest, most barriers disappear. It has to be made clear that the user and beneficiary of the developed system is not going to be an anonymous "company," but they themselves. They will be able to access the experience of their colleagues and solve problems they could not solve before, as well as end situations in which colleagues constantly pester them for advice. The resulting help-desk system will enable them to work with increased efficiency and effectiveness.

Apart from the help-desk operators, management has to be motivated as well. CBR is perceived to be rather academic by most managers. While to them investing resources into a database project seems to be no problem, investing into CBR is investing into a venture with an uncertain outcome. It has to be clarified that CBR is an established technology and by no means only an academic playground. It also has to be clarified that the initial installation of the case-based help-desk support system is only the beginning of a process that will enable the company to capture and reuse experience. Management must be prepared to invest resources on a continuous basis while the system is operational. A CBR system is only useful if it contains knowledge and is being maintained on a continuous basis.

Without continuous management support and employees who are willing to fill and use the system, any CBR project is bound to fail.

**CBR Tool Selection.** Based on the project, domain, and user-group specifications, a suitable tool to develop the case-based help-desk support system must be selected. Criteria to be taken into account include:

- the operating environment in which the system is going to be used (hardware and software, network architecture, database type, and so on),
- the complexity of the technical domain (home appliances or networked workstations),
- the level of experience of both the end-users and the help-desk operators,
- the organization of the help-desk (number of levels, physical locations, and so on),
- the project goals that have been defined.

Since the case-based help-desk support system is going to serve as a (long-term) knowledge repository for the organization, this selection should be based not only on technical criteria, but also should take into account economic and organizational considerations, as well as strategic decisions of the company.

### 7.2.3 Organizational Processes During System Development

**Project Team and Initial Domain Selection.** The creation of a project team to serve as the "knowledge engineers" and the selection of a group to serve as initial test users of the system are the first organizational steps that must be taken.

Apart from the person implementing the case-based help-desk support system (*CBR consultant*), the project team should contain help-desk personnel who are very experienced in the relevant subdomain to be modeled and well respected by the help-desk operators outside the project group. Personnel that are interested in "technology" rather than implementing useful systems are very common in help-desk environments, but definitely not helpful in creating a case-based system and should be avoided. Once selected, the members of the group should be kept constant, i.e., fluctuations should be avoided.

The group of initial users should comprise two types of help-desk personnel: One that is on a comparable level of expertise with the project team with respect to the selected subdomain (i.e., expert users) and help-desk personnel who are less familiar with the specific problem area (i.e., novice users). While the expert test-users can communicate to the project group in their language, the novice users will represent the target group for which the system is being implemented. Feedback from both types of users is required for a successful project. After a first "rapid prototype" has been implemented, the expert users can give hints regarding problems with the knowledge modeled in the system. The members of the novice user group, on the other hand, will serve as models of the help-desk operator who will use the system. The vocabulary in which the cases are being represented and the knowledge contained within them has to be adjusted to the novice user group

Which domain one selects for the initial knowledge acquisition is of utmost importance. The domain should be representative of the problems that are being handled at the help-desk, both in terms of complexity and frequency. It should also be a problem area that accounts for a considerable amount of the workload and about which the help-desk operators are interested in sharing (obtaining) knowledge.

**Training the Project Team.** Training the project team is an organizational process that has a major impact on the success of the help-desk project. At the beginning of the project, the project team is (most of the time) inexperienced with respect to CBR and knowledge acquisition. Since the project group will be responsible for system maintenance and continuous case acquisition after the development has finished, it is very important that they are trained in CBR, as well as in knowledge acquisition and modeling, during the initial knowledge acquisition.

While the project team should also get advanced training to be able to model, fill, and maintain the knowledge in the system, the test users only need to be trained in using the resulting case-based help-desk support system.

**Development of the Knowledge Acquisition and Utilization Processes.** The introduction and use of a case-based help-desk support system usually causes a re-evaluation and modification of the existing knowledge and information management processes in a help-desk environment. When the system is used, it must be integrated into the operating environment of the help-desk operators and become part of the standard business process. Existing processes must be altered to facilitate the flow of information to and from the CBR system. When organizational processes are defined, the tasks to be performed, the personnel or roles to perform these tasks, and the communication among the groups/roles have to be fixed.

After the development of the case-based help-desk support system is complete, it will serve as the central source of information for the help-desk operators. To ensure a smooth flow of information, the knowledge sources and formats, as well as the qualification of the personnel that requires the knowledge, have to be analyzed, and processes that allow efficient and effective acquisition and use of knowledge have to be developed. One should keep in mind that while the group enacting the initial knowledge acquisition process is the project team and rather experienced, the users who use the system in the end (both in terms of knowledge retrieval and continuous acquisition) may be less qualified.

During the development of HOMER (see section 3.1), we found it very useful to define three roles for the organizational processes during the use of the help-desk system:

— the help-desk operator,
— the CBR author,
— the CBR administrator.

Help-desk operators are the users from the target group. Their duty is to use the implemented help-desk system in their daily work. If they cannot find an appropriate solution with the system, they will have to solve the problem on their own and generate a new case. Depending on the domain and on managerial decisions, this new case may or may not be made immediately available as an "unconfirmed" case to the other help-desk operators. For maintenance purposes, the operators are also encouraged to comment on the quality and applicability of the cases in the case base.

The unconfirmed, new cases have to be verified in terms of their correctness and suitability for the case base by the CBR author(s). The CBR author is a person with experience both in the domain and in using the CBR system. While the CBR author can decide on the quality and inclusion of a case in the case base, he or she is not allowed to perform modifications on the vocabulary, the similarity, and the adaptation knowledge. These can only be performed by the CBR administrator.

The personnel enacting the roles of the CBR author(s) and the CBR administrator should be included in the project group from the start of the project. It should be noted that both these roles require a considerable amount of resources and should be performed by dedicated personnel. If the organization or the size of the help-desk does not permit dedicating more than one person to these tasks, the duties of the CBR author and CBR administrator should be performed by one person.

### 7.2.4  Technical Processes During System Development

**General IT-System Development Related Processes.** The development of a case-based help-desk support system is similar to any other IT project in most aspects. As usual, the system has to be specified, implemented, integrated, and verified. The definition of the requirements, the implementation, and the testing and revision of both the prototype and the actual case-based help-desk support system are steps that have to be performed in accordance with standard software engineering techniques. However, the user-interface and the connection to supporting programs (integration) are two features that require additional attention.

The essential task in developing a user interface is to present the relevant data, at the right moment, in the right representation, and on a level of abstraction that is suitable for the current users of the system. If the available data is presented to the users in a way that they do not understand, in a representation they are not familiar with, or at a moment when it is irrelevant, it will only cause confusion and be of no use. While the exact specification of the firmware installed on a printer may be necessary information for a second-level help-desk operator, it will be rather useless for a first-level help-desk operator who is just trying to figure out whether the printer is connected to the computer. The user interface of the case-based help-desk support system has to be developed in accordance with the user group (i.e., second level, first level, or even end-user), the specific domain, and company policies (who is allowed to see what kind of data). It has to present the right data, at the right moment, on the right level of abstraction, and in accordance with company policies.

A case-based help-desk support system cannot operate in isolation. While the CBR system will store experience, it will not contain data regarding device configurations, maintenance contracts, and users. Maintenance information and device configurations are stored in an inventory system most of the time. Data regarding the end-users is usually stored in another, separate database. Since this information is needed during problem solving, the system has to have interfaces to these databases.

Most help-desks use trouble-ticket tools in their daily operations; they record, manage, trace, escalate, and analyze the calls they receive. While these trouble-ticket tools are very useful in handling calls, they do not provide means to capture and reuse problem-solving experience. Depending on the environment, the case-based help-desk support system should also either be integrated into the user interface of the trouble-ticket tool or vice-versa. Data from the trouble-ticket system has to be transferred to the CBR system to initialize the attributes that relate to the data that has already been acquired. Except for very complex second-level applications, it is not feasible to have two points of entry to the problem-solving process.

**Initial Knowledge Acquisition for the Case-Based Help-Desk Support System.** A CBR system is useless without cases. When the case-based help-desk support system is handed over to the help-desk operators, it has to contain enough cases to cover at least part of the relevant problems at the help-desk. Otherwise the system will be considered useless and the project will fail.

Initial knowledge acquisition serves three major goals:

- training the project team in knowledge acquisition,
- initializing the knowledge in the system,
- collecting enough help-desk cases to bootstrap the system.

During initial knowledge acquisition, the knowledge in the system can be distributed among the *domain model* (vocabulary), *similarity measure, adaptation knowledge*, and the *case base*. These *knowledge containers* (Richter 1998) have to be created and filled. While the similarity measures, the adaptation knowledge, and the vocabulary are compiled knowledge, the case base is interpreted at runtime. In principle, each container could be used to represent most of the knowledge. However, this is obviously not very feasible, and the CBR consultant should carefully decide on the distribution of knowledge into the containers. After the initial knowledge acquisition is completed, this distribution is more or less fixed and should only be changed with caution.

The processes for the acquisition of knowledge for each container run in parallel and cannot be easily separated during the initial knowledge acquisition. Since the vocabulary lays ground for entering the cases and describing the similarity measures and adaptation knowledge, it has to be available first. However, to be able to create a domain model (i.e., the vocabulary), one has to understand how the domain is structured, and this can only be done by looking at the cases, the similarities, and the adaptation rules.

In our experience, the best way to approach this problem is to create and use standardized forms to acquire an initial amount of cases from the project team. The form should be developed in co-operation with the project team. A sample form that was developed for the initial case acquisition for the HOMER (cf. section 3.1) application is shown in Tab. 7.2.

The first thing that must be done is to ask the project team to fill out as many case acquisition forms as they can. By looking at the elements of the forms, the vocabulary (i.e., the phrases that have to be used and the domain structure) can be derived and a vocabulary that is capable of describing the cases that have been on the forms can be modeled.

By asking the project team what the range of possible values for each attribute on the forms is and inquiring what would have happened if one of the values on a form were different, a broad range of cases can be created and the vocabulary expanded in a short time. Discussions among the project team members raise the level of understanding of both the approach and the problems, and should be encouraged in this early phase. One should also keep in mind that the goal is not to model the domain in every detail but on a level that helps the system's user solve a problem (i.e., the system does not have to solve the problem autonomously). Especially during initial knowledge acquisition, it is advisable to have more cases on an "everyday" level rather than having a few extremely specific ones.

**Tab. 7.2.** Sample form for initial case acquisition.

| Homer Case Acquisition | |
|---|---|
| **Problem Nr : 0816** | **Date: 26.04.99** |
| **Author:** S. Itani | **Verified by:** J. Fleisch |
| | |
| **Problem Description (Failure)** | Printer does print pages full of gibberish |
| **Reason (Fault)** | File is Postscript, Printer does not understand PS |
| **Solution** | Send File to Postscript Printer, delete file from queue |
| | |
| **What did you check to find out what the problem was ?** | |
| Printer Model | HP LJ 6L |
| File Type | Postscript |
| | |
| | |
| **Other Notes:** | The reverse of this problem did also happen, somebody sent a PCL file to a pure PS printer |

While the initial vocabulary is being created and value ranges fixed, questions regarding adaptation rules and similarities should be posed and the results entered into the system.

One of the major challenges one must face when creating a system to capture and represent the experience of domain experts, is determining the level of abstraction with which the domain and the knowledge will be modeled. If the model used is too simplistic, it will cause problems while the experience is being captured and will miss important details. If, however, the domain model is too specific, the user will get lost quickly in useless details, and knowledge acquisition will be very tedious and time consuming. Maintenance is very difficult for both a too-simplistic and a too-complex model.

The decision to use a structured domain model approach as opposed to a textual query-answer-based approach also depends on the system's intended users. For inexperienced help-desk operators, a tool with which simple problems can be solved by answering a limited number of questions is of great value (Thomas et. al. 1997). However, for experienced help-desk operators who would not bother to use a system for (subjectively) trivial problems, a structured domain model approach yields better results. The system will be able to present the not-so-obviously similar solutions that the help-desk operators could not find. Since knowledge contained in the domain model is used in similarity calculation, the retrieved solutions will be similar in a semantic and structural manner. The domain model allows the solutions in the case base to be applicable to a broader range of problems.

The cases in the help-desk domain should be modeled in accordance with the approach the help-desk operators use in solving problems (Fig. 7.1).

The *Problem Description* is the first information the help-desk operator gets from the end-user. This description is what the end-user subjectively perceives as the problem. It may or may not have to do with the actual cause of the failure.

The *Diagnosis Path* consists of the questions the help-desk operator must ask or the information he or she must obtain from various sources to arrive at a diagnosis. The diagnosis path contains the minimal amount of information that is necessary to diagnose the problem.

The *Solution* contains the fault, i.e., what caused the problem, and the remedy, i.e., how to solve the problem. Depending on how the system is implemented and what statistical information is needed for further evaluation, some additional, administrative data may also be added to the case description.

Each complete path from problem description to solution makes up one case.

Once the cases from the initial forms have been entered into the help-desk system, the system should be shown to the project group to verify the results it delivers. Afterwards the initial knowledge acquisition can continue as more cases are entered from additional forms and the knowledge containers are incrementally updated.

Initial knowledge acquisition takes place in two steps. During the first, preliminary knowledge acquisition, the cases for the prototype of the case-based help-desk support system are collected. While the collected cases will help to initialize the knowledge containers and train the project team, the collection of the "core" cases for the system should be done in a second step, the core knowledge acquisition. Nevertheless, the approach that is used in both processes is similar.

## 7.3  Using the System

### 7.3.1  Managerial Processes During System Use

Project progress with respect to the qualitative and quantitative criteria selected as project goals must be monitored constantly during system development and use (cf.

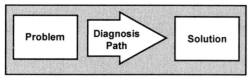

**Fig. 7.1.** Basic structure of a help-desk case.

Stolpmann & Wess 1999). Regular project reviews should take place. Standard project planning and controlling techniques can and should be applied to case-based help-desk support projects.

Measuring the impact of the help-desk system on the efficiency and effectiveness of the target group (increase in first-call problem resolution, decrease in problem solution time, and so on) and making the results available to both the project and the target groups will motivate the help-desk operators to use the system and help uncover deficiencies.

### 7.3.2 Organizational Processes During System Use

**Knowledge Utilization and Acquisition Process.** The knowledge utilization and acquisition processes that have been defined during system development have to be enacted during system use. The use of the case-based help-desk support system contains the Application Cycle in which the system is used by the help-desk operator and the Maintenance Cycle in which the system is maintained by the CBR author and the CBR administrator (see section 7.3.3, Fig. 7.2).

During the application cycle, the cases that are stored in the case-based help-desk support system are being used to solve problems. Even if no new cases are being acquired during this cycle, statistical data regarding the quality and usage of the cases (last retrieval time, last application date, success rate and so on) can be collected. This data can be used to determine the quality of the cases and for maintenance purposes.

Whenever a help-desk operator decides that the proposed solution is not appropriate, a new case has to be entered into the case base. However, since the quality of these cases varies according to the user entering them, they cannot be transferred to the case base without being verified by the CBR author. This is done in the maintenance cycle. The extension and maintenance of the case base is the duty of the CBR author and the CBR administrator.

**Training the Help-Desk Operators.** Just as the test-users were trained during the project team training, the help-desk operators have to be introduced to the basics of CBR technology and the developed case-based help-desk support system. Since the operators are going to participate in the continuous acquisition of knowledge, standards on how to store cases have to be introduced and taught. Feedback-channels also should be created and introduced during this training.

### 7.3.3 Technical Processes During System Use

**Continuous Knowledge Acquisition and Maintenance.** The knowledge contained in a case-based help-desk support system is an incomplete model of the domain in the real world. Whenever the real world changes, the model in the

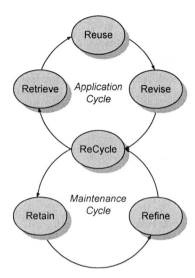

**Fig. 7.2.** Use of the case-based help-desk support system.

system has to be updated. The necessity for changes in the model may either arise from real changes in the world or from the learning effect associated with using the case-based help-desk support system. By learning, the system improves the model's coverage of the real world. Since the model is incomplete by definition (and no such thing as a closed world exists in the real world), with growing knowledge, updates in the knowledge containers will be necessary.

While nobody would consider purchasing a database system with the assumption that it would continue to work without any maintenance at all, there seems to exist a misconception about knowledge-based systems in this respect. All concepts used for maintaining database systems are also applicable to knowledge-based systems. However, because of the semantics associated with the information in knowledge-based systems, additional maintenance operations are necessary. Learning and changes in the real world can make maintenance necessary for each knowledge container.

A case-based help-desk support system comprises two linked process cycles: the *Application Cycle* and the *Maintenance Cycle* (see Fig. 7.2).

The *Application Cycle* takes place each time a user solves a problem with the case-based help-desk support system. During the application of the CBR system, the standard tasks *Retrieve*, *Reuse*, and *Revise* must be performed (see section 2.6). During *Retrieval* the most similar case or cases in the case base are determined based on the new problem description. During *Reuse* the information and knowledge in the retrieved case(s) is used to solve the new problem. The new problem description is combined with the information contained in the old case to form a solved case. During *Revision* the applicability of the proposed solution (solved case) is evaluated. If necessary and possible the proposed case is repaired. If the case solution generated during the reuse phase is not correct and cannot be repaired, a new solution has to be generated by the help-desk operator. The solution that has been retrieved by the system or created by the help-desk operator is put to use during the *Recycle* task. The *Application Cycle* is performed by the end-user of the system (help-desk operator).

Whenever a new solution is generated during system use, this case is stored in the case buffer, made available to all help-desk operators as an "unconfirmed case", and sent to the *Maintenance Cycle*. These operations as well as the maintenance cycle are not visible to the standard help-desk operator.

The *Maintenance Cycle* consists of the *Retain* and *Refine* tasks. While the *Application Cycle* is executed every time a help-desk operator uses the CBR system, the *Maintenance Cycle* can be executed less frequently, i.e., only when there is a need for maintaining the system or at regular intervals.

During the *Retain* task, the CBR author checks the quality of the new cases that were generated by the helpdesk operators and stored in the case buffer.

The CBR author verifies and approves the representation and content of each case. In terms of representation, the cases should

- contain the information that is necessary and sufficient to solve the problem,
- be described on an abstraction level that is appropriate for the system's end-user.

The content is verified by checking whether the case is

- correct,
- (still) relevant, and
- applicable.

During the *Refine* phase, maintenance steps for the knowledge containers are performed by the CBR administrator. The case base, vocabulary, similarities, and adaptation knowledge have to be refined, and quality-decreasing effects of external changes in the domain, as well as the inclusion of new cases in the case base, have to be counteracted.

The goal of the *Refine* task with respect to the case base is to keep the case base correct, to have maximal coverage of the problem space, and to have no redundant cases. After each case has been validated in the retain task, their suitability for inclusion in the case base has to be determined.

Before a new case is taken into the case base, it must be checked to see

- whether it is a viable alternative that does not yet exist in the case base,
- whether it subsumes or can be subsumed by an existing case,
- whether it can be combined with another case to form a new one,
- whether the new case would cause an inconsistency, and
- whether there is a newer case already available in the case base.

The operations that have to be performed during case base maintenance vary depending on the application domain and the vocabulary that is used to represent the cases.[1]

Both the inclusion of new cases and changes in the domain may have an effect on the validity and quality of the compiled knowledge containers (vocabulary, similarity, adaptation knowledge) as well. The maintenance of these containers is also performed in the *Refine* step. Since changes in the vocabulary can cause information in the cases to be no longer available or missing (e.g., attributes can be added and deleted, classes can be moved) maintenance of the vocabulary should be performed with utmost caution (Heister & Wilke 1998).

It should be noted that the refinement of the knowledge containers does not necessarily have to be triggered by external events but may also be performed through introspection. By analyzing the content of the knowledge containers, more efficient ways to structure the domain, adaptation rules, and similarities, as well as new cases, can be discovered or derived.

While maintenance operations for the case base can be performed by the CBR author, maintenance of the vocabulary, the similarity, and adaptation knowledge should only be performed by the CBR administrator.

**General IT-System-Related Processes.** Once the case-based help-desk support system has been put into operation, it has to be debugged, monitored, and updated continuously. The necessity for updates does not necessarily have to come from the help-desk system itself, but may also be initiated by changes in the (IT) environment. Since these processes are not CBR-specific but apply to IT systems in general, we refrain from going into their details here.

## 7.4 Process Model for a Help-Desk Project

The overall process for the development and introduction of a case-based help-desk support system can be divided into six main phases.

— project planning and initialization
— implementation of a rapid prototype
— evaluation and revision of the prototype
— implementation of the integrated case-based help-desk support system
— evaluation and revision of the case-based help-desk support system
— utilization of the case-based help-desk support system

During *Project Planning and Initialization*, the preliminary requirements for the execution of the project are fulfilled. The project goals are defined, the project

---

[1] See Leake & Wilson (1998), Smyth & McKenna (1998), Surma & Tyburcy (1998), and Racine & Yang (1997) for details.

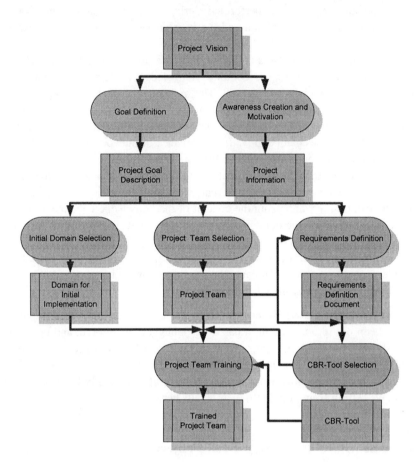

**Fig. 7.3.** Project planning and initialization.

information is disseminated, the project team is created and trained, and the CBR tool is acquired (Fig. 7.3).

The *Implementation of the Rapid Prototype* enables the project team to test the validity of the goals and the requirements set forth in the project-planning phase. It also serves to train the project team in knowledge acquisition techniques and in using the CBR tool. The processes that will be used during knowledge acquisition can be defined and refined. The "Rapid Prototype Implementation," "Preliminary Knowledge Acquisition," and "Knowledge Acquisition Process Development" processes are closely interconnected and influence each other. While changes in the prototype will effect the way knowledge is acquired, changes in the domain model will effect changes in the acquisition process as well as the user interface of the system, and so on (Fig 7.4). The interaction between processes is shown with dotted lines in the figures.

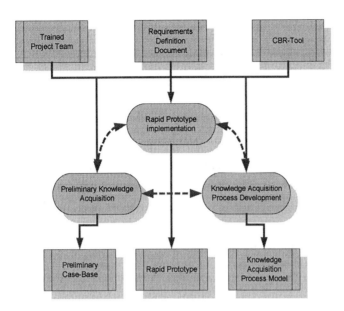

**Fig. 7.4.** Implementation of a rapid prototype.

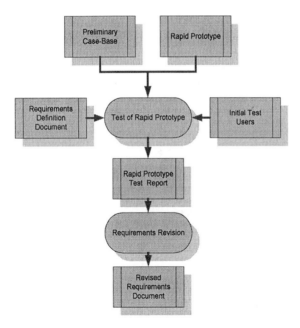

**Fig. 7.5.** Evaluation and revision of the prototype.

During the *Evaluation and Revision of the Prototype* (Fig. 7.5), the initial users (see section 7.2.3) evaluate the developed a rapid prototype as well as the structure and content of the knowledge containers. The results are collected in a revised-requirements definition document, which serves as a basis for the development of the actual system.

The *Implementation of the Integrated Case-Based Help-Desk Support System* contains the development of the actual system to be used at the help desk. The implementation is based on the preliminary case base, the revised requirements, the rapid prototype, input from the project team, and the process model for knowledge acquisition. While the system is implemented, the project team acquires the core-case base to be deployed with the system after implementation is complete. The processes to be used when the system is used are also developed in close connection with the implementation and the knowledge acquisition in this phase (Fig. 7.6.).

During the *Evaluation and Revision of the Case-Based Help-Desk Support System* the system is evaluated by the initial users and revised according to the results of this evaluation (Fig. 7.7.).

The system is put to use in the *Utilization of the Case-Based Help-Desk Support*

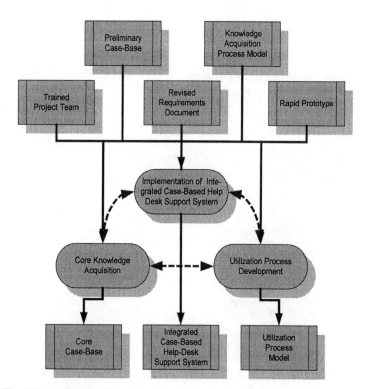

**Fig. 7.6.** Implementation of the integrated case-based help-desk support system.

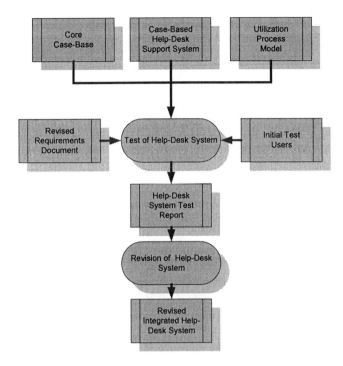

**Fig. 7.7.** Evaluation and revision of the case-based help-desk support system.

*System* phase. The impact of the system is continuously monitored and feedback is given to developers and users (Fig. 7.8).

## 7.5 Impact of the Methodology in Developing and Using Help-Desk Support Systems

The process models shown above were created during the development of the HOMER application (see section 3.1). One of the goals of the implementation of HOMER was to observe and record the processes that have to be enacted during system development and use. The results of these observations have been documented as a *recipe* in the *cookbook* level of the INRECA methodology. The process models shown above have been extracted from this recipe. Full details can be found on the INRECA CD-ROM.

In the course of developing the methodology, we documented the tasks that were performed, their duration, the resources needed, and the outcome of the tasks. While monitoring our own actions, we discovered redundancies as well as dependencies among processes that were not obvious. This enabled us to structure,

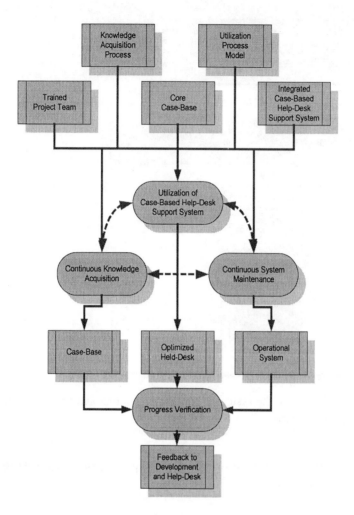

**Fig. 7.8.** Utilization of the Case-Based Help-Desk Support System.

optimize, and understand some of the processes better. Even the development of the methodology had an impact on the way the project progressed.

After the process models were complete, the methodology and the developed tools were used during the *project definition, application development,* and *system utilization* phases of new projects. As described in chapter 5, the methodology has an impact on *productivity, quality, communication,* and *management decision making.* We could observe the advantages of using the methodology in each of these areas and in all three project phases, both to the customer (management and user) and to the developer.

### 7.5.1  Impact of the Methodology During Project Definition

During the definition of a project, the processes to be executed have to be detailed. For each process, this involves defining the methods to be used, the project's duration, the resources needed, the results to be produced, the interaction with other processes within the project, and the sequence in which the processes must be executed.

By means of the methodology we were able to create project definitions with structured process models, task definitions, roles and responsibilities, duration, and resource allocations. The methodology enabled us to make the case-based help-desk support system development process traceable both to the customers and to ourselves.

While the creation of the project definition for HOMER from scratch took us about three months, we were able to reuse the help-desk recipe to define three new projects in less than a week each. The overall duration of these projects varied between six months and three years. Since we reused a recipe that had been executed before, we could be sure that all aspects that needed be taken into account were covered. Since the basic "recipe" was available, we could concentrate on the peculiarities of each domain. The quality and level of detail we were able to achieve in these project descriptions were far beyond the level that can be achieved when a description is created from scratch.

Apart from these advantages in increased productivity and quality, the methodology was also very useful for communicating with the customer and conveying the message that the development of a CBR system is not an art, but, rather, solid technology. As we mentioned above, Case-Based Reasoning is still considered an academic approach by some managers. Being able to describe each process in the development of a case based system in detail enabled us to convince managers of the validity of the approach, clarified the need for continuous maintenance and resource allocation, and let us raise realistic expectations. We were able to give customers figures on how much effort had to be spent by whom and when. Project progress became measurable. This gave them a basis for making decisions, enabled them to plan their resource allocation in advance, and prevented the loss of critical resources in the course of the project.

### 7.5.2  Impact of the Methodology During System Development

The detailed project plan that was created during project definition served as a guideline during the development of the system. The ability to trace a structured path and the use of the software tools that was developed to support the methodology allowed us to speed up the development process by a factor of 12. While the development and testing of the first prototype in HOMER and comparable applications took up to six months from the initiation of the projects, we were able to create a prototype and test it at another site of DaimlerChrysler within two weeks.

Since the tasks that have to be performed and the results that have to be achieved during the implementation of the system were described in detail in the "recipe" and the project definition, some tasks could be transferred from one developer to the other without additional effort, and the progress that was achieved during the project could be measured. A clear-cut definition of the tasks to be performed and the availability of tools for creating and maintaining a domain model allowed us to use less-qualified personnel during the development of the system without compromising the quality of the resulting product. This allowed both the developer and the customer to optimize the allocation of personnel resources.

### 7.5.3 Impact of the Methodology During System Use

During the development and initial use of HOMER, we had to define and modify the tasks and qualifications of the personnel needed to operate the system several times. Since the processes for the acquisition, use, and maintenance of the knowledge in the case-based help-desk support system are defined in the methodology, we were able to introduce new help-desk systems in a much more efficient manner. While the domain modeling and maintenance task could only be performed by a highly qualified help-desk operator in the HOMER project, the domain modeling and model-maintenance tools, as well as the similarity editor that was developed to support the INRECA methodology, enabled us to use much-less-qualified personnel in the ensuing projects.

The detailed definition of the duties that have to be performed and the qualification that is needed for the project group also enabled the customers to allocate the necessary resources in advance and monitor the status of the project according to the goals that had been set when the project was initiated.

The methodology was also used to train users in the administration of a case-based help-desk support system. Using process charts, we explained the overall structure of the project to the operator who would be in charge of the project after it was completed. This allowed the operator to maintain and use the system without getting lost in details and neglecting important aspects, like maintaining the case base.

## 7.6  Conclusion

To develop case-based help-desk support systems that will be used in dynamic, corporate environments by a large group of users, one must take into account the managerial, organizational, and technical processes. It has to be kept in mind that once a CBR system is in place, continuous knowledge acquisition and maintenance is necessary. Processes for knowledge acquisition and maintenance have to be developed and put in place, and personnel have to be dedicated to performing these tasks.

The processes necessary to develop a case-based help-desk system have been described in a recipe of the cookbook level in the INRECA methodology. The methodology structures the development and use of case-based help-desk systems, makes it transparent, traceable, and its success measurable. Using the INRECA methodology in the project definition, system development and system utilization phases of new projects resulted in considerable increases in productivity and quality. The methodology also provided a means of communication and served as a basis for management decision making.

# 8. Developing Intelligent Catalog Search Applications

This chapter describes the recipe for building catalog search applications that incorporate Case-Based Reasoning. The concept of finding a solution to a problem based on the similarities between the new problem and recorded cases in a case base is central to the CBR approach. When developing an intelligent catalog search application we simply treat the product list as the case base and the user's requirements for a product as the new problem. The recipe for building catalog search applications, therefore, shares many of the characteristics of help-desk and classification applications. We will describe the detail of the recipe and how the methodology has impacted on the practical issues associated with building a new application.

## 8.1 Characteristics of an Intelligent Catalog Search Project

In recent years, the traditional paper-based publishing of product or service catalogs has given way to the electronic delivery of catalog information. CD-ROM allows an organization to deliver a more functional catalog for a much lower production and delivery cost than could be derived from a weighty paper-based catalog. The Internet extends this to support the delivery of up–to-the-minute product information to the ever-increasing Internet population and, in turn, can capture valuable market information from the online use of the catalog. The problem faced by companies who use electronic catalogs has changed from "How do we efficiently get our information to users?" to "How do they use it when they get it?"

The main problems users experience can be summarized by the following statements, familiar to all catalog users: "Results 1-10 of 426, "Please refine your search," and finally "Sorry, no match found!" The technologies whose applications generate these messages are equally well known, i.e., **databases**. Commercial relational databases support Boolean (yes or no) queries. In other words, if the database doesn't have exactly what you want, then it has nothing that you want. Similarly, if it has many items that meet your request, then it presents them as a list without ranking. The last one in the list could be the ideal product to meet your needs. The approaches to catalog searching most commonly used are: keyword search, stepwise search, and parametric search.

**Keyword search.** This is the most basic and generally the least effective. It relies on matching words entered by the user with words contained in the product specification or description. For example, if a user is searching a database of properties and types *Washington* in the keyword search, he or she may get properties in Washington State or Washington, D.C, properties near an airport with regular flights to Washington, properties for whom the agent is John Washington Realty, and many more than we can imagine.

**Stepwise Search.** Stepwise Search presents a hierarchy of product categories to the user. The user gradually refines the search by going deeper into the product tree. Yahoo[1] is an example of such a search on the Internet, and Krakatoa ™ (Neal 1997) from Cadis Inc. provides a tool for developing such systems for CD-ROM and Internet catalog searches.

**Parametric Search.** This kind of search is common and is often combined with keyword or stepwise searches to improve functionality. In this approach, the user enters one or more values for attributes of the product. Attributes of parameters can generally be numeric or symbolic. A parametric search acts like a filter and is, in effect, the same as a database query; it either meets all search criteria exactly or it

---

[1] See www.yahoo.com

fails. Some parametric search systems provide ranges and sets of values to overcome the limitations of the database approach, but still "No match found!" is a common occurrence. Some implementations of this approach use the product code and manufacturer's code as the parameters, which means that the user must know the product he/she wants before starting the search. Ouch!

The fourth approach, and the subject of this chapter, is the *Nearest Neighbor* method of searching, also called *Intelligent Parametric Search*. This approach is a key output from CBR research and is the basis for the INRECA Catalog Search applications. The characteristics of the problem domain that make "nearest neighbor" so effective are as follows:

— users need to search the product space in its entirety,
— products in the product space will be similar is terms of their characteristics and their structure,
— the user generally does not need an exact match; the optimum match will suffice,
— the user needs the ability to *negotiate* with the search system,
— no match found is an unacceptable outcome from a search (i.e., "sellers want to sell.")

Human assessment of similarity or closeness is a normal thinking function and in many cases an automatic one. A sales person interacting with a customer in a real scenario will not take the customer's requirements as absolute unless told so by the customer. The sales person will treat these requirements as a goal or ambition for the customer and will try to establish the customer's priorities before making a recommendation. This allows the customer to give a precise statement of requirements but not have it interpreted as such. The *intelligent parametric search* does exactly this and uses weights to represent user priorities.

## 8.2  Vertical Platform for Catalog Search

Through experience in building a variety of catalog search applications that make use of CBR technology, we can now define a *vertical platform* for this type of application. The platform describes the tools and methods used to build an intelligent catalog search application, as well as the characteristics of the eventual end-user system.

### 8.2.1  Case Structure and Domain Model

In general, the case structure for a given application is defined by the product specifications in the existing catalog or in the available product literature.

Therefore, the case structure is well known in advance, since it relies on an existing set of products whose characteristics are known (contrary, for instance, to a diagnosis application where one must make an intensive effort to "discover" the domain model).

In many cases we have found that a *flat* structure is sufficient to meet the search needs of most end-users. By *flat* we mean that all attributes of the product of interest are used to describe every product in the catalog. The alternative to a flat structure is an *object* structure. As an example, an object structure for a car might see its attributes as [body, engine, wheels, electronics] where body would contain [color, style, doors, and so on] and engine would contain [cc, fuel, hp, and so on], while a flat structure would contain [color, style, doors, cc, fuel, hp, and so on], all at the same level. The *object* model allows us to describe a structure for a more complex product representation, and this is supported by the CBR tools. However, an object model structure means a more complex interface for the user, and this, unless necessary, should be avoided. A flat representation can simplify the user's view of the catalog search and in most cases give the same level of functionality as the object representation. A flat model also can be stored easily in a standard database system, of which many are available.

The process of defining the domain model involves specifying and applying data types for each of the catalog attributes. Basic data types are:

- Boolean,
- Date,
- Integer,
- Real,
- String,
- Symbol.

These attribute types may need to be specialized to cater to the needs of a specific project. As an example, in the Analog Devices search application, the Temperature Specification for each device can be listed, in a simplified way, as one of [Commercial, Industrial, Military, Space]. The order of these values is important, as it demonstrates an increasing scale of Temperature Specification. Therefore, in this project we created a type "Temp_Spec_type", which is an ordered symbol with the set of possible values defined as shown in Fig. 8.1.

### 8.2.2 Defining Similarity

The assessment of the similarity between one product and another, and indeed between one value for a parameter and another, is always likely to be subjective. The expert's view of similarity will differ from the customer's, and, as a result, the effectiveness of similarity calculations is best seen in the appropriateness of the results. In each of the intelligent catalog search applications developed to date, it

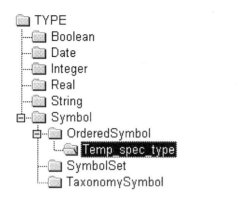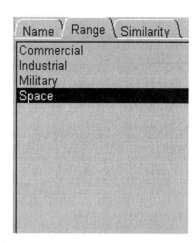

**Fig. 8.1.** Creating a specialized type.

was necessary to go through a process of experimentation with the similarity functions. In other words, standard (simple) similarities did not work, and a set of tailored similarity functions had to be defined. See section 3.2 for an overview of the Analog Devices application.

### 8.2.3 Customer Dialogs

The dialog with the customer is the key to a successful implementation of an intelligent catalog search application. Some questions need to be answered before a developer can prepare the dialogs to support the customer in using the search system. Does the customer need to weight the parameters for which he or she specifies values? What validation is required for inputs to the search? What explanation of the search parameters is needed? What explanation of the results is needed by the user? What extra features will the user need to make use of the query or results featured in the system? Each of these questions is important, and the answers can only be obtained by consulting users directly or by consulting people who deal with user queries on a daily basis. As a consequence, the catalog application should be open to validation based on feedback from its use in the "field." This step is important to ensure the catalog's long-term acceptance and success.

### 8.2.4 Integration with Product Database

The product database, if it exists, is a starting point for the creation of a catalog search system. The CBR system can use the database directly in two ways:

1. to generate the index for the nearest neighbor search. This index uses only the parameters from the database that are relevant for the search. The creation of the index involves combining the model, data, similarity measures, and pre-defined weights into a fast, searchable structure. When the database changes, this index must be regenerated to include the new products or items in the catalog.

2. to display the results of the search. On completing a search of the case base, the search returns a reference to a record in the database that contains the detailed product information and link to literature, if required. On the Analog Devices CD-ROM, this is used to launch Adobe Acrobat and load a detailed data sheet of the electronic device of interest. On the IRSA Expertise search it is used to load an Active Server Page with details of the scientist and links to his or her personal Web pages (see Fig. 8.2).

### 8.2.5 Web Interface

The Web opens up enormous possibilities for the presentation of product information to an international customer base. At the moment, most Web sites provide basic database or keyword searches that in many cases reflect negatively on the Web site because of poor-quality search results. The capability of the nearest neighbor search to use all parameters and still return a result means that Web interfaces can now be more dynamic and supportive to the user.

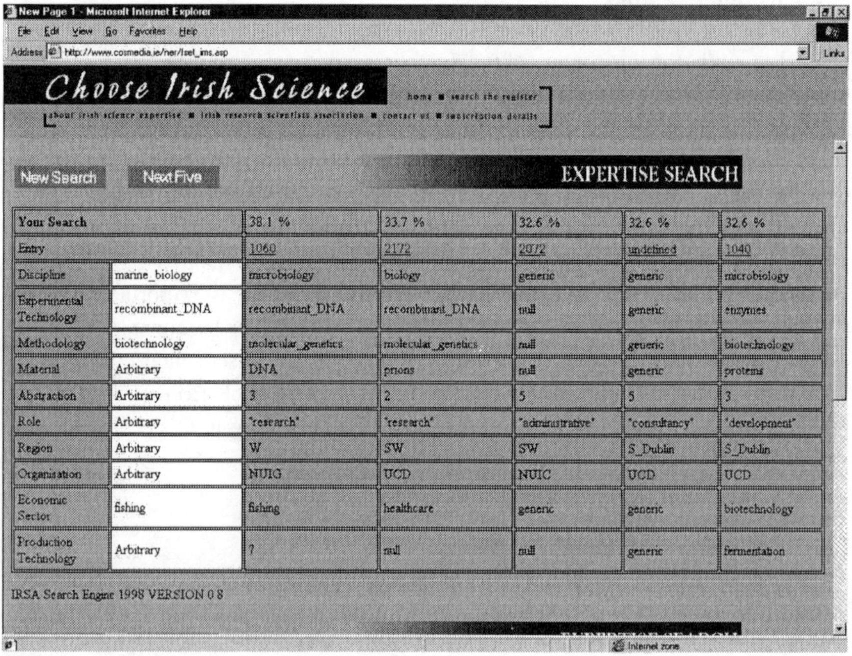

**Fig. 8.2.** IRSA search results dialog on the Web.

Instead of discouraging the user from specifying all his or her needs, we can encourage the user to "tell all." The impact of this is that, following a search using CBR, we have a log of the detailed requirements from each user. Over time, this log represents invaluable market information and a basis for reviewing the product catalog contents and presentation.

Web interfaces to the intelligent search server can be created easily in HTML, Active Server Pages, XML, or Java. The INRECA project has produced tools to support the creation of these interfaces.

## 8.3 Process Model for Catalog Search

The recipe for developing catalog search applications breaks down into five main processes linked as shown in Fig. 8.3. These processes are now described.

### 8.3.1 Requirements Acquisition

The process of acquiring the user and business requirements for the catalog search application involves three key activities: analyzing technical and sales materials, eliciting user requirements, and, finally, eliciting business requirements (cf. Fig. 8.4).

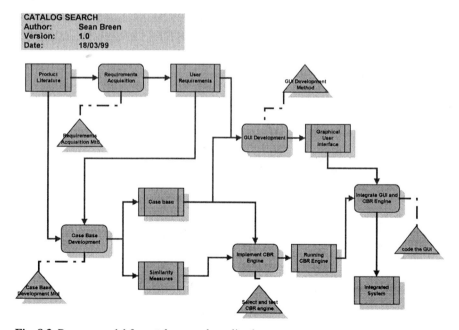

**Fig. 8.3.** Process model for catalog search application.

**Analyze Technical and Sales Materials.** An analyst knowledgeable in data modeling and CBR should be assigned to gather and review all available materials used internally or externally to describe the products or services of interest. Material may be available in several forms: product database or catalog, sales literature, technical data-sheets, design specifications, and Web documents. It is possible that the detailed information in these forms will conflict. We have noticed that sales literature often presents a simplified view of the product specifications, making it unsuitable for an experienced or knowledgeable customer.

**Elicit User Requirements.** The intended application user ,or stake-holder, should be interviewed and asked to describe the following:

 — current work practices in the application area,
 — perceived problems or areas that need improvement,
 — his or her vision of what the best possible situation would be,
 — his or her relationships with other staff members in and out of the area.

From a practical point of view, the team of people involved in this process should include an analyst knowledgeable in data modeling and, ideally, in CBR, a sales person from the company who provides the products or services listed in the catalog, and a technical person who understands the makeup and specifications of the products or services under discussion. The sales person is expected to have an understanding of the customer's needs, the ways in which they currently use company information when selecting a product, and the best way to meet their needs using a CBR catalog search application. The technical person is expected to

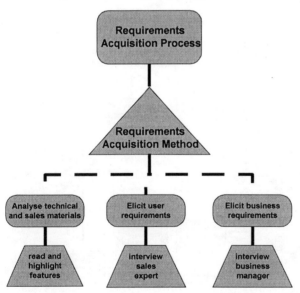

**Fig. 8.4.** Process decomposition for requirements acquisition.

be in a position to describe how individual products or groupings relate to each other functionally and how values for individual parameters or attributes can be compared to each other. The analyst will interview each of these professionals and use the information to establish the data and interface requirements for the catalog search application.

**Elicit Business Requirements.** Sales support is a key business function, and the input of an experienced business manager to the creation of an electronic sales support application is essential at this stage in the process. Many possibilities exist to enhance the sales process when a decision is made to create a CBR Catalog Application. An experienced business manager will be in a position to highlight these opportunities and to make the business case for focussing on them during the course of development.

### 8.3.2  Case Base Development

Development of the case base is a three-stage activity: descriptive model development, similarity development, and case acquisition (see Fig. 8.5).

**Descriptive Model Development.** This will draw on the outputs of the requirements acquisition process to define a list of attributes and organize these into a class hierarchy. Different tools may provide for different types of data and will certainly have different ways of implementing the descriptive model. It is important to ensure that the tool you choose to implement your application supports the model you have describe.

**Similarity Development.** This is not broken down in this diagram, since it is a well-developed, common generic process to almost all CBR projects. See the INRECA CD-ROM for further details. See also (Bergmann & Stahl 98).

**Case Acquisition.** This is essentially either a manual input operation or a question of importing existing data. Importing electronic versions of the case base is certainly the most likely scenario in a product catalog application; however, there may be a procedure put in place that allows for manual additions to the case base once the initial import is done. CBR tools such as Kate and CBR-Works both support importing cases from database or ASCII files, and both support the CASUEL (Manago et al. 1994) case format defined by INRECA.

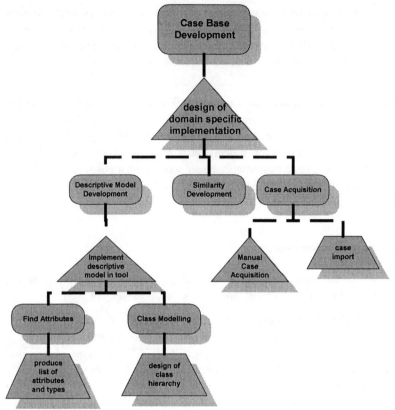

**Fig. 8.5.** Case base development process decomposition.

### 8.3.3  GUI Development

The development of a Graphical User Interface (GUI) for your catalog application is likely to consume a large part of the development work for your project (see Fig. 8.6). This is where the technology meets the technophobe.

An application without a user interface designed for real users will almost certainly run into problems when it goes live. This is not wisdom gleaned from CBR projects but a broadly accepted IT maxim: "Ignore the user at your peril." Where possible, involve users early in the design of the GUI. Get their feedback when creating the graphics for the application and show them screen-shots of the eventual system. These actions will prompt questions regarding the functionality of the system that will be much easier to deal with at the start of a process than at the end. Formal acceptance testing should be conducted at the end of the GUI development to sign off on the interface before integration of the CBR component begins.

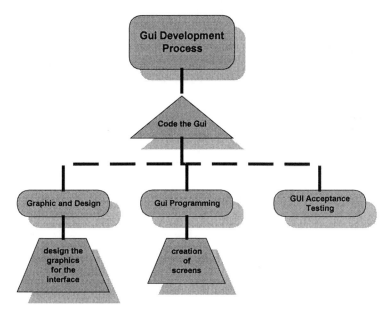

**Fig. 8.6.** Graphical user interface development process.

### 8.3.4 Implement CBR Engine

The engine that drives the catalog search application is obviously a key component (cf. Fig. 8.7). Specific questions should be answered by the engine's supplier before a final decision is taken to adopt one nearest neighbor search facility over another.

— Is the product scaleable: what limitations exist for the number of cases, and how is performance affected as the case base grows?
— Does the engine support changes to the model once the application has been deployed?
— Are there limitations to the number of users?
— Are there restrictions on the number of case bases that can be used?
— Are there clear separations among the model, data, and similarity measures?

### 8.3.5 Integrate CBR and GUI

The CBR engine and GUI components are integrated to form a single application (see Fig. 8.8). This step is not trivial and often requires experimentation and tweaking to get the application to work. An experienced developer may be required to solve any issues relating to the differences between the GUI environment and

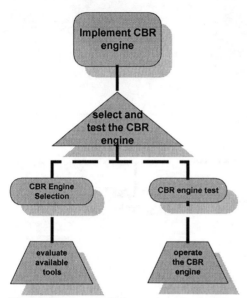

**Fig. 8.7.** Implement CBR search engine process.

the CBR engine environment. The system should, of course, be fully tested in its component and integrated forms. Testing should approximate, as closely as possible, the ways in which actual users will interact with the system. Testing at this stage may raise issues that lead to changes in the model or similarity functions within the system. The final step in deploying the system is to implement the links to the existing product data or literature. This will be trivial if the links are facilitated through an existing catalog database, as was the case in the IRSA and Analog Devices applications (see annex A and section 3.2).

## 8.4  Benefits of the Methodology

The partners involved in developing the INRECA methodology have developed, among them, over 15 catalog search applications using CBR. The first four of these were used to formulate the initial version of the "catalog search application" complex method, and subsequent applications were used to enhance and refine it. The impact of the methodology on the later applications and its expected impact on future applications can be described as follows:

**Development Time is Shortened.** The impact here has, in at least one case, been very dramatic. The first Analog Devices search component took six months to produce, the second six weeks and the third only two days. Some of this is due to automation, but much is due to the systematic reuse of a proven method.

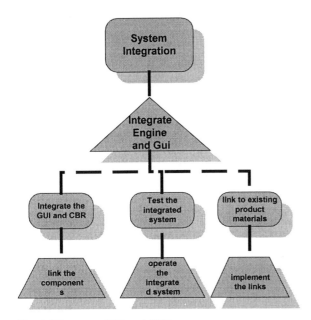

**Fig. 8.8** Integrate CBR and GUI process.

**New People Can be Introduced Quickly.** Documentation of the process allows us to quickly bring new people up to speed. We have an independent record of experience and clear documentation on how to apply it.

**Steps in the Process have been Automated.** By formalizing a record of the method we use, we have been able to identify steps in the process that are suited to automation, and we have developed computerized versions of these processes.

**Customers Like the Comfort Factor.** In any innovative domain, it is important that the customer be comfortable with the concept and the risks involved. A clear method removes the feeling that "black magic" is involved, and the business decision becomes easier for the customer.

**Clear Documentation is Maintained.** Many software quality systems require a systematic documentation regime before approval is granted. The INRECA methodology, when fully applied, generates high-quality and highly usable documentation that meets this need.

# 9. Developing Maintenance Applications

"Data is a burden, knowledge is an asset." Operators and manufacturers of complex equipment often collect data about the equipment they maintain: technical follow-up files, breakdown files, intervention reports, preventive maintenance reports, and records of requests from their clients or distributors. Unfortunately, this information is usually not well exploited. This is due both to the complexity of the equipment itself and to the type of technicians who carry out the maintenance processes. In this chapter, we explore a recipe for this category of problems, with a specific case structure and modeling approach, as well as typical problems for linking the developed maintenance system to both on-board equipment and technical information.

## 9.1  Characteristics of a Maintenance Application for Complex Technical Equipment

A typical piece of complex technical equipment shows a high degree of dependence between the different modules or parts that compose it and its different organs. Typically, this modern equipment contains electronic systems. Some examples of such complex equipment to be maintained are:

- traction and brakes on streetcars,
- on-board computer systems on high-speed trains,
- oil systems on aircraft engines,
- pistons on large marine diesel engines,
- robots.

For these kinds of equipment, a decision-support system typically provides:

- an action to carry out,
- a spare part to replace,
- some technical documentation to consult.

### 9.1.1  Typical Input and Output

Maintenance actions are usually done by experienced technicians. The data the maintenance support system uses is generally accessed by the technicians either directly (by querying the equipment database directly), or after they have performed an action suggested by the system. This information can be in the form of:

- information extracted from the current state of the equipment itself,
- data extracted from the current session (by communicating with the equipment),
- data extracted from the history of the equipment, or
- information provided after the technicians have carried out some actions.

The input parameters have to be defined jointly with the equipment specialists. These can be:

- the state of the equipment when the fault has been noticed,
- the state of the equipment in the past,
- the actions carried out by the technicians to identify the fault.

The output parameters will cover:

- the action to perform,
- the part(s) to replace,
- the technical documentation to consult.

### 9.1.2  Technical Characteristics

The main characteristics of building a diagnostic application for the maintenance of complex technical equipment are:

— Because of the complexity of the equipment, failures are rarely identical. Additionally, there are a high number of possible different failure patterns. A systematic approach for tracking all possible failures and the conditions under which they might appear is, therefore, not possible. Some foreseen failures will never happen, whereas failures that were not planned will be observed frequently.
— The end-users of such a diagnostic system are qualified technicians. They have very specific knowledge. There is no knowledge base available. Indeed, they do not describe the problems in a deterministic way but with their "feelings," based on their experience.

Moreover, because the equipment is technical, it has specific characteristics. Technical equipment is becoming increasingly modular. The same parts of a system can be used in many configurations. For instance, an electronics card can be reused in different parts of a train, or even on several different trains. Hence, it is necessary to develop a specific diagnostic process for this card. However, since the diagnostic procedures depend on each other, it is necessary to plug the card into the general framework of the whole piece of equipment. In fact, a typical piece of technical equipment is often composed of smaller subsystems, which themselves are decomposed in order to reach the Line Replaceable Units (LRUs). An aircraft engine, for instance, is composed of major modules (low-pressure turbine, fan and booster, combustion chamber, and so on), themselves decomposed into minor modules (bearings, rings, and so on) and finally into LRUs (sensors, cables, and so on). Figure 9.1 represents such decomposition.

This organization has major consequences for the diagnostic process:

— the modeling process must take into account the reusability of the subsystems,
— the cases must share information among different models,
— the retrieval process has to help the user navigate among the different subsystems.

Another typical characteristic of complex technical equipment is that they often interact with the computer system. For instance, on-board avionics can provide information about the state of each component, as well as automatically provide data requested by the user (maintenance personnel). As a consequence, the diagnostic system has to be ready to receive two categories of information: One provided automatically by the equipment (self-diagnostic, and so on), and one provided after investigation by the technician. Both types of information will significantly move the diagnostic process toward either a black-box style (fault trees if most of the information is automatic) or an open style (dynamic CBR consultation if most of the information has to be asked of the end-user).

Finally, integrating the diagnostic process into a powerful information system is an absolute necessity. Indeed, technical drawings, IPCs (Illustrated Parts Nomenclatures), service bulletins, job cards, and so on, help the technician either correctly apply the recommended procedure, or, simply, understand the behavior of the equipment.

## 9.2 Vertical Platform for Maintenance

As we have seen in the previous paragraph, maintenance of complex technical equipment requires specific procedures for modeling the data, collecting the cases, defining the diagnostic process, and integrating the process into the end-user environment. For instance, trial applications by TGV maintenance technicians have demonstrated that the number of attributes increases quickly with the number of functions covered. When creating the cases and building the fault trees, if any, the technician has to take into account all of these attributes for each reference case. Most of these attributes are not relevant for the subsystem considered. However, the technician has no way of knowing this in advance. Thus, if the case base is broken into smaller chunks corresponding to subsystems with their own case bases, it is difficult to maintain the case base and the data model, and it is difficult to use the case base because the many attributes make the choice harder for the technician.

This section describes the development processes related to building a technical maintenance application. It focuses on the description of the hierarchical data model (section 9.2.1) and on acquisition of the cases for each case base of this hierarchical data model (section 9.2.2).

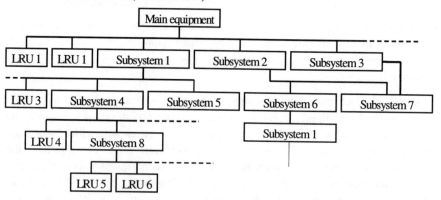

**Fig. 9.1.** The decomposition of a complex piece of equipment.

### 9.2.1 Domain Model: The Hierarchical Approach

The difficulty of maintaining complex technical equipment comes mainly from the difficulty of understanding the impact of a failure from a specific organ on the equipment's functions. In general, a single organ has an influence on several different functions. When a technician troubleshoots a fault in the equipment, he or she perceives the functional consequences of an organ failure: One or several functions are affected.

The general principle of building hierarchical models aims at splitting a complex model into $n$ simple submodels. Each submodel may itself be decomposed into other submodels until it becomes a simple model, with fewer than 15 attributes, which are easy to maintain. Adding a new attribute is done in only one submodel and does not impact existing cases that are related to other subsystems. The submodels are reusable and can be called from different functions. The input used for defining the functional decomposition of the equipment is:

— Functional specifications of the equipment (decomposition in major, then minor modules). These specifications describe the associated fault codes and the associated context.
— The organs themselves enable the technician who builds the hierarchical model (let us call him the "expert"), to refine this functional decomposition when organic fault codes, like autotests, etc., exist.

Figure 9.2 shows the proven process model for building hierarchical domain models. The main steps for building the model hierarchy and the content of each model are summarized below:

— The first step is to define the data model hierarchy which is based on an analysis of the existing information on:
  • functional architecture,
  • data supplied by the equipment,
  • additional observations made by the technician.
  This is the starting point for describing more precisely each submodel within the hierarchy and the common attributes among the models.
— For each model in the hierarchy, it is then necessary:
  • to create the data dictionary that contains the technical sentences used to describe a case,
  • to define the attributes and attribute values,
  • to test the data model. This can be done by integrity tests ("Do any cases have a value in a submodel for any attributes?" "Are there no conflicts between two models that have common attributes?" And so on.), by study of completeness (for instance, "Does a submodel cover all the possibilities of failures for a specific LRU?"), and so on.

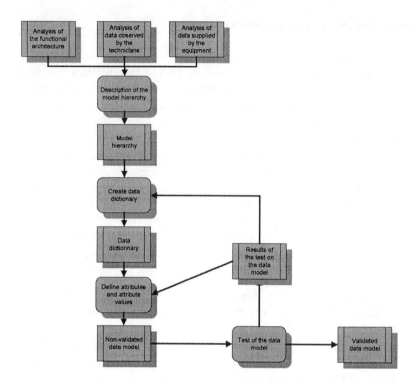

**Fig. 9.2.** Process model for building the hierarchical models.

### 9.2.2  Case Acquisition Process

The processes related to case acquisition are strongly linked to the definition of the hierarchical data model. The information collected during the previous phase enables the experts to refine the initial decomposition. The "electronic" data (fault codes, contexts, and so on) will allow the expert to create high-level case bases for each main function. This initial case base will guide the technician towards one of the subfunctions that are related to the main function.

**Example.** For a TGV, the main case base concerning "Opening access doors" contains sufficient information to guide the technician towards:

−   a problem with the whole train (problem on the on-board computer network),
−   a problem with a specific door.

Because of the hierarchical modeling, each case base is simple enough to be described in a relational way, i.e., a matrix where each line corresponds to a case and each column corresponds to an attribute value (electronic information or question to the operator). Each case concludes either with a final diagnosis or with a submodel. There is generally no need to build a complex interface for creating and validating the cases.

The different steps for building each case base are (see Fig. 9.3):

— definition of the database structure related to a submodel. The result of this process is a physical database structure,
— definition of the authoring environment (a simple one the technician who creates the cases can directly update). Once the authoring environment is ready, the technician uses it directly to author the cases,
— creation of the current case base. Typically, the technician will use two sources of knowledge: The one that comes from the technical information about the equipment (analytical information) and the one that comes both from his experience and from the historical behavior of the equipment (practical information). As a consequence, the technician will author two categories of cases:

  • analytical cases,
  • real cases.

Even when authoring real cases, it will be necessary to analyze them in order to verify that they are complete and coherent. For both analytical and real cases, it is necessary to describe the solution. It may be either a final diagnosis, or a link to another case base. These cases are then saved in the database of current cases, which contains cases not yet validated.

— validation of the cases. This validation can either be done:

  • manually, by reviewing each case and comparing it to the other cases of the case base. This is possible since each submodel is small and the case base is dedicated to the diagnostics of a specific subsystem of the considered equipment,
  • automatically, by building a fault tree. The fault tree can help the technician discover holes in the case base or discover incoherence between cases,

— transfer of validated cases. The last step is to transfer the validated cases from the current case base to the reference case base.

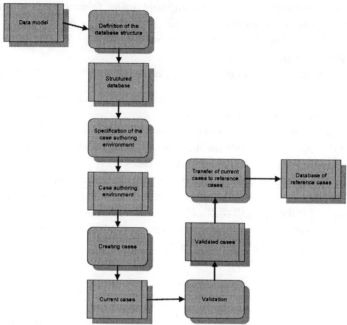

**Fig. 9.3.** Process model for case acquisition.

When the case bases are being built, some rules also apply so case retrieval can be optimized:

– About the case base as a whole: each case base must be modular. It should be possible to use it independently from the other case bases and to make it evolve without interacting with them.

– About the cases themselves:

  • Each attribute has to have at least two possible values in the case base.
  • For each case, each attribute should have a value
  • A case may have several conclusions, since it is sometimes difficult to define an attribute that discriminates among near solutions.

## 9.3  Impact of the Methodology in a Maintenance Application of Complex Technical Equipment

Because of the complexity of the equipment, the technicians often rely on their own experiences to solve a failure, and they have difficulties transmitting this experience to their colleagues. The hierarchical domain model approach together with the INRECA methodology that describes how to build those hierarchical models allows this complexity for the description of problems and their solutions to be reduced. As a consequence, the introduction of the INRECA methodology has positive impacts on:

— the productivity of the building process,
— the quality of the results obtained,
— the communication among the members of the development team,
— the monitoring of the development process.

### 9.3.1 Productivity for Building a Diagnostic Support Application

By productivity, we mean the reduction of the effort necessary to reach the desired result. A high productivity is ensured by applying this recipe, which enables the developer to easily build a hierarchical domain model because:
— The maintenance effort of the system is low. An updated specific data model or case base has no impact on the other models or case bases.
— Authoring the case and maintaining the data model are simple enough because of equipment decomposition. Authoring and maintaining can be mastered by the technicians themselves. This reduces the delay in obtaining and maintaining the cases and models.

A typical example of the productivity increase was demonstrated when the TGV application was built (see section 3.3). A first attempt at data modeling and case base authoring was made in three months for describing problems related to a "chain of traction" of the TGV (the set of equipment required for maneuvering the train). Four experienced technicians were first trained on data model and cases authoring tools over eight days. Then they started to describe the data model and the cases related to this chain of traction. After three weeks, they decided to stop because the number of cases began to grow exponentially as they started to analyze the subparts of the chain of traction. Consequently, the development process was modified. By applying the updated development process, one technician was then able to provide a first set of data models and the corresponding case bases (29 different models) in less than two weeks.

### 9.3.2 Quality of the Results Obtained

Applying the INRECA methodology increases the quality of the results obtained because:

— the decision support process is documented and reusable,
— the best specialists can be hired to describe complex subsystems they know well, since the amount of work is lower.

For instance, in the TGV application, it was necessary to match some internal ISO-like quality plan. The application of the INRECA methodology enabled the client to more easily validate the results. Each part of the application (each data model, each case base, and so on) could be validated independently and could demonstrate a better quality than when everything were mixed up. This was possible because the specialists needed much less time to achieve the same work and, as a consequence, paid much more attention to it.

### 9.3.3 Improved Communication

Documenting the processes lets users not only improve and validate the results, but it also improves communication among the development team members, and between the development team and the end-users (By "development team, we mean people who author the cases and data models). This improved communication has two benefits:

- Understanding the content of the data models and the case bases is much better because of their granularity. Each case base and each data model is small. As a consequence, everybody has the same understanding of its content.
- The documentation of the diagnostic process improves the understanding of the CBR technique itself. This is very important for the acceptance of the technique. Let us move back to the example presented in section 9.3.1. The technician who authored the case bases in fewer than two weeks told us that he had finally understood the need and the behavior of CBR after he had read the documentation about the diagnostic process. This example can be generalized. Many maintenance technicians are use to representing what they know or want to learn, through flow diagrams. Since the INRECA methodology proposes the same approach for describing the CBR development processes, it is easily understood and improves the communication and the understanding within the development team.

### 9.3.4 Managing Decision Making

The INRECA methodology offers a solid basis for management decision making: Planning, resource allocation, and monitoring. It allows the managers to create project plans with structured process models, adapted task definitions, roles and responsibilities, duration, and resource allocations. By defining and documenting the process models, the methodology ensures that every aspect is taken into account when a new CBR application is developed. It makes the development process transparent both to the customers and to the developers. It is a key point for the managers when they decide whether to start a CBR project. By offering proper processes, by documenting each level of the processes, and by closely defining the input and output of each part of the processes, the INRECA methodology helped the CBR tool developer convince the customers of the validity of this approach. It clarified the need for data models and case base maintenance and allowed the managers to estimate precisely what resource allocations were needed based onto realistic expectations.

For the TGV application, applying the INRECA methodology also helped convince managers that the service technicians could handle the development of many different case bases (several hundred). It was possible to quantify the resource allocation for creating and maintaining this information, and to precisely define roles and responsibilities for each task. Finally, the INRECA methodology helped AcknoSoft, as a CBR service provider and tool vendor, to more accurately estimate provisional efforts and delays, produce a reliable project plan and write a clear proposal which was then accepted by the client.

# A. Compilation of INRECA Methodology Applications

## A.1 ALSTOM – Improving Train Availability to Optimize Operating Cost

*With KATE, we have developed an innovative diagnostic tool that allows us to offer high-quality, after-sales service. Our initial experience with the product has allowed us to integrate the maintenance aspect from the beginning--when we respond to a call for tenders--which represents a true competitive advantage.*
Pierre Dickeli, Business Development, Customer Services

With over 24,000 employees worldwide, Alstom is one of the world's leaders in the transportation market, whether for trains, subways, street cars, or its renowned high-speed train, the TGV. Located in the Paris region, the company's Department of Electronic Equipment Systems (EES) designs and manufactures all of the electronics equipment and information systems embedded in its transport vehicles. Such embedded electronics are becoming ever-more important, because they not only improve train performance, but security and energy consumption as well.

One of the key factors in reducing vehicle operating costs is to increase their availability, which means improving vehicle reliability and accelerating diagnostics when the vehicles break down.

To create a new computer-aided maintenance system, Alstom engineers studied several technologies for developing a reliable and evolutionary diagnostic tool: Expert systems, Case-Based Reasoning and model-based reasoning. Finally, they chose AcknoSoft's KATE, which integrates CBR and induction techniques into a single tool.

Being able to create a diagnostic system that is flexible and able to enrich its own knowledge base over time were key factors in Alstom's decision. The diagnostic tool is available for Alstom's customer service division on portable PCs and on its Intranet, thanks to KATE-WebServer. It is used 24 hours a day by the transportation operators' maintenance crews.

The generic computer-aided maintenance system can be adapted to any type of transport vehicle and associated electronics equipment. While a train is in circulation, its embedded electronics equipment continually receives data on the train's functioning, which can be transmitted in real time to the maintenance center. Thus, when the train breaks down, the maintenance center is alerted to the dysfunction even before the train arrives at the station platform. The diagnostic tool, which compares the transmitted data to cases from previous breakdowns in its database can identify the best maintenance procedure for the problem.

In addition to saving maintenance time, this ambitious project, which has been achieved with the help of maintenance specialists and train conductors, enables a true transfer of knowledge.

## A.2 ANALOG DEVICES – Sales Support for Integrated Circuits

*For the past ten years we have tried, like our competitors, to develop a satisfactory parametric search engine that would help our pre-sales people. With two-feet thick catalogs describing thousands of ICs, finding the right product or the closest to the customer's needs is not an easy job, even for a well-trained engineer. We tried CBR and in less than a year we had a unique and successful presales tool.*

David Kress, Director of Applications Engineering, Analog Devices

With sales of $1.2 billion for fiscal year 1996, Analog Devices is a leading provider of precision, high-performance integrated circuits used in analog and digital signal processing applications. Analog Devices designs, manufactures, and markets a broad line of high-performance linear, mixed-signal, and digital integrated circuits. Headquartered in Norwood, Massachusetts, the company employs more than 7,000 people worldwide and has manufacturing facilities in the United States, Europe, and Asia.

With thousands of products, Analog Devices was, until now, printing catalogues and data sheet up to two feet thick each year,! The cost of printing and shipping catalogs to its 50,000 customers worldwide approached $3 million per year.

Most of Analog Devices's products within a product line differ from each other by only one element. And they can be described by up to 50 parameters! Technical support presales engineers take the customer's requirements over the phone and try to find a match in the Analog Devices product range, a complex process that involves weighting dozens of constraints while at the same time interacting with the customer, usually a design engineer, to try to understand his, or her, real priorities. This lengthy process can be successfully accomplished only by well-trained engineers.

For the past ten years, Analog Devices, like its competitors, tried to solve this problem with half a dozen software projects using standard database management system. But this approach was not very helpful, since SQL-style searches only return a value when all conditions are met exactly. When a customer provides a complete set of specifications, the most likely answer is "no match," and, when he or she relaxes some of the specifications, hundreds of matches are found.

The solution was provided by Interactive Multimedia Systems (IMS) using KATE's Case-Based Reasoning technology. Using "nearest neighbor matching," IMS developed a working prototype in fewer than 6 months.

Called parametric search, the system allows customers to specify interactively their product requirements, then finds either the right product or the product as close as possible to their needs. With this system, the customer enters the specifications directly onto the screen. Values can be numbers or information, such as "the best," "sort of" or "less than,"

The parametric search system always provides an answer: A list of the top ten Analog Devices's products that are closest to the specified requirements. If the user is not satisfied, another search can be started with new priorities until the right product is found.

The parametric search is now available on Analog Devices' operational amplifiers and will soon cover data converters. Available to customers on a CD-ROM catalog, the parametric search system is also used by the pre-sales engineers on their Intranet. It will soon be accessible through the Internet, as part of the Analog Devices web site[1]. Analog Devices is expecting a savings of $2 million this year, since the cost of producing and shipping 120,000 CD-ROM is far less expensive than producing the paper version.

But it is the quality of the service parametric search system provides that makes the difference in this very competitive market. Now when customers call sales support, they usually know exactly what they want, and order exactly what they need. For the support engineer, this means having more time to concentrate on truly complex customer requirements. Because the system can keep track of the customers' requests, a future extension of the system will analyze this valuable marketing information and use it to design new products.

## A.3 ANSALDO – Maintaining the Metro in Naples

*An advantage of CBR, particularly compared to rules, is that the knowledge base can be very easily updated. Thanks to CBR, we produced a tool that allows maintenance staff who do not have specialized skills in computer science to update almost the entire knowledge base.*
Antonio Ruggieri, Ansaldo Trasporti

In Southern Italy, the Circumvesuviana Railways have operated the busy railway lines of Naples' suburbs for over one hundred years. With a usual life span of 40 years for a train, the cost of maintaining the 200 vehicles is critical.

---

[1] http://www.analog.com

According to the Italian Railway Company, the maintenance costs for electric traction vehicles represents 60% of the life cycle cost of a locomotive, which is much more than the acquisition cost, even at $3 million a piece! And increasing the availability of railway vehicles not only reduces maintenance costs, but also minimizes the number of vehicles needed.

Using AcknoSoft's KATE, an innovative diagnosis system was developed by a team of engineers from the Circumvesuviana Railways and the manufacturer Ansaldo Trasporti, with help from the University of Salerno. CBR technology was preferred to the rule-based methodology because it is easier to implement and because the knowledge base could be easily updated by the maintenance staff who are qualified technicians but not IT specialists!

This 16-man/month project has produced a working system for use by first intervention teams and maintenance shop workers. Because diagnostic equipment might be used on a train, the system runs on a laptop computer with a standard multimedia hardware configuration. It is also available on an Intranet with a web interface. First the user describes the warnings given by the instrument panels. If this information is not sufficient to identify the failure cause, the diagnostic system prompts the user for more information. Verification of the damaged system is done through a sophisticated hypermedia interface. The system can provide pictures, sounds (such as a breaker noise), and movies to describe possible failures. In the final phase, a diagnosis and the intervention process are given to the user. Reducing maintenance costs was the main objective for developing a new diagnostic system, but there are other positive effects, such as improving the multidisciplinary expertise of operators.

## A.4 CENTRE NATIONAL D'ETUDES SPATIALES – Optimizing the Reliability of Ariane

*The combination of data mining and Case-Based Reasoning techniques allowed us to develop experiential applications in the most effective way possible.*
Luc Brégeault, Technical Division, Matra Systems & Information

While Ariane Espace handles marketing for Europe's Ariane rocket, its launch operations are the responsibility of France's National Center for Space Studies (CNES) in Kuru, French Guyana, for which Matra Systems & Information (MS&I) acts as system integrator.

In the past, to guarantee an operational site every three weeks for the current Ariane launch schedule, CNES relied on a database of 10 years worth of incident data: 17,000 incidents recorded, with 1,500 new ones added every year. Until now, this mass of precious information was used by quality managers, with the help of statistical tools, to determine that all systems were good. While such tools were perfect for providing quantitative information, they were incapable of locating a solution to a previously experienced incident.

Intrigued by the idea of integrating inductive, Case-Based Reasoning technologies into the database, as well as KATE's capacity to manage complex data, MS&I used KATE to develop, in six man-months, a diagnostic system for quality assurance officers. Based on a description of a current incident, the system instantly locates all similar incidents from the past, a task that once had to be accomplished by a manual search through thick printouts.

The system's ergonomically designed user interface accepts natural language queries. Based on portable PCs, the system will soon be deployed for Kuru's 50-person Quality and Maintenance Department team.

## A.5 DAIMLERCHRYSLER – The Intelligent Hotline

*Our hotline operations rely on the knowledge and the experience of experts. CBR-Works helps us to utilize this human capital efficiently and effectively.*
Thomas Pantleon, CAD/CAM Support, DaimlerChrysler AG

Daimler-Benz sees itself as a first-class provider of vehicles in all automotive market segments. The outstanding worldwide reputation of the Mercedes-Benz brand will continue into the next millennium based on new and innovative products.

Within its passenger car development department, Daimler-Benz uses more than 1,200 UNIX workstations for CAD/CAM, while running more than 20 different software applications. Hotline operations and customer service costs are high in this area. At the Sindelfingen, Germany, locations alone, 600 complex problems have to be solved monthly.

Outstanding customer support is a key to successful competition. Since products and services are growing more and more complex while at the same time changing rapidly, the cost of this service is becoming increasingly high. Therefore, efficient decision-support systems are needed for customer support.

The advantage of the CBR approach is in the collection and intelligent provision of experience. CBR-Works takes customers' problems and compares them to already-known problem cases. When there is no direct solution, the user is guided interactively to a new one. The availability of this asset for every hotline employee drastically reduces the time required to process a request. By applying CBR technology to their hotline operations, Daimler-Benz expects yearly savings of nearly $600,000 for passenger and utility cars.

HOMER is part of the ESPRIT project INRECA II and has been implemented jointly with the Daimler Benz research department in Ulm, Germany, by tecInno. The productive use of the system started at the end of 1997.

## A.6 GICEP ELECTRONIQUE – Diagnostic Help for Circuit Boards Used in Halogen Stove-Tops

*Our objective was to reduce our maintenance costs and the number of difficult repairs required, and to save 20% off our repair time. Today, the user no longer needs to search the notebook for difficult cases; they are accessed directly in the system, which acts as a memory aid.*

Serge Bossé, I.T. director, Gicep Electronique

Located near Angers, France, Gicep Electronique is a small company specializing in repairing complex electronic circuit boards, including those used in halogen stove-top burners.

Though only a hundred odd such boards are processed each week, their problems are among the most difficult to diagnose. For this repair activity to be profitable, workers must find the cause of the malfunction and fix it in fewer than 45 minutes. If they can't, the boards must be labeled "difficult to repair" and set aside. Then, to find the information necessary to fix the unit, a worker must search for a similar malfunction in the company's repair history notebook .

To reduce the maintenance costs and repair time of this procedure, Gicep used AcknoSoft's KATE-CBR to develop a diagnostic tool in fewer than three months. Of the 4,000 types of malfunctions cataloged, the company initially chose 200 representative cases to introduce into the case base. Another 50 odd, which are being validated, will soon be added. Operational since September 1996, the system tells the worker which repair to undertake, based on a description of the malfunction's symptoms. Particularly user-friendly, the system then displays a diagram of the board with the exact location of the defective component. Less than a year after  the system's installation, Gicep is highly satisfied; the system has provided a return on the investment in six months and the desired reduction in repair costs. For the repair team, being able to share the know-how of scarce experts has improved overall team performance, allowing the team to make difficult repairs even when the experts are absent.

## A.7 IRSA – Expertise Knowledge-Base

*CBR has allowed us, for the first time, to provide a real search facility for scientific expertise. This is a real advance for the overseas promotion of Irish Science sector.*

John Donovan. Secretary Irish Research Scientists Association (IRSA)

The Irish Research Scientists Association maintains a database relating to the qualifications and expertise of its membership. Until recently, this was only searchable using a standard keyword procedure. The usefulness of this, however, was limited by the variable levels of detail in the entries, which were produced by the members themselves. The information about individual scientists relates to their discipline, experimental technology, research interests, and much more. Since individual scientists use different terms to refer to the same area, a keyword search was of little use. As a result, the aim of this application was to provide a consistent "fuzzy" parametric search facility that would be available to:

— college-based agents responsible for managing the interface between research and industry,
— industry-based R&D managers seeking recruitable postgraduate expertise or expert consultants,
— government agencies seeking to expedite the emergence of a healthy R&D community.

The facility runs on the Internet and provides the following search parameters to the user:

— discipline
— experimental technology
— methodology
— material
— level of abstraction (theoretical to practical)
— role of the Scientist
— economic sector
— production technology
— broad location
— organization identity or type

The results the system generates are ranked according to how similar they are to the user's enquiry, and links are included to the scientist's detailed record, which may further link to a personal or departmental web site.

At the time this book was being written, the site had been in operation for a few months, and a strategy for growth and revenue generation for the facility was being planned.

## A.8 LEGRAND – Rapid Cost Estimation for Plastic Parts Production

*We chose KATE because our target users preferred the Case-Based Reasoning approach, which is less bothersome to use than rule-based systems. Our development teams appreciated the speed and ease of the product's installation, as well as the support from AcknoSoft.*
Jean-Nicolas Manas, Project Manager, Service Production Department, Legrand

With over 19,000 employees worldwide, Groupe Legrand is the market leader for low-voltage electrical equipment. Whether destined for the housing or service industries, or specifically designed for industrial uses, Legrand products cover nearly every conceivable function of low-voltage electrical installations: Switching and branching, protection and repartitioning, current distribution, communication, and security. As new product-line life cycles continue to shrink rapidly in response to an evolving market, Groupe Legrand has made the reduction of time to market its main priority.

A major part of low-voltage electrical equipment is its plastic components. At Legrand's Limoges site alone, over 200 thermoplastic injection molds are produced every year, and its plastics production experts are in great demand.

So the company's Center for Studies and Research in Plastics Science in Limoges, France, in collaboration with AcknoSoft, developed the Rapid Cost Estimation for Plastic Parts Production (ERCP) system. The result of 10 man-months of development, ERCP allows technicians to determine the cost of tooling investments and the wholesale price of the finished part at the outset of its development cycle. Capitalizing on the know-how of company specialists, the system's case base contains the detailed characteristics of over 600 tool configurations. Each case comprises over 40 pieces of data, including photos and CAD drawings. Designed with the help of plastics production and pricing experts, the project facilitated communication and a real knowledge transfer between the two sectors. Over time, the system will enable pricing experts to estimate the cost of a part in three days compared to three weeks, reducing by 30% the total cost of work required by specialists. The application may be adapted later for estimating the costs of metal parts, and KATE may also be used to develop a system for disseminating manufacturing data to design engineers.

## A.9 MET-ERICSSON – Analyzing Telecommunication Cards and Electronic System Test Data

*The rapid evolution of electronic card technology makes diagnosing faults ever more difficult and delicate. Introducing a knowledge-based system that uses induction and Case-Based Reasoning techniques has provided us with promising new perspectives.*

Jean-Luc Dieusaert, PBA's Test Engineering & Maintenance,
Quality Department, MET-Ericsson

MET, a subsidiary of Swedish telecom giant Ericsson, faces a critical dilemma in its manufacture and installation of public telecom network equipment, notably central telephone switches, or PBXs. At its plant in Longuenesse, in the northern French region of Pas-de Calais, MET must reduce the cost of testing and diagnosing faults in equipment so complex that acquiring experience with it is difficult.

Diagnosing why an electronics card does not work properly is particularly representative of the problems MET employees face. The complexity of a card increases in direct proportion to the greater number of functions it provides and the number of components mounted on its surface. Methods for testing the cards have evolved along with the card technology itself, but following the path of the signal and getting information on individual components during the diagnostic phase have remained extremely delicate tasks.

Furthermore, the diagnostic time allotted to technicians at the plant has declined significantly, caused in part by shorter product life cycles. Because of time constraints, the process of diagnosing and repairing cards today can make or break a card manufacturer, since the components on a card can represent over 90% of the finished product's resale price.

In 1997, MET's quality division launched a study on how to improve its diagnostics, and it launched its first project using AcknoSoft's tool KATE a few months later. The system employs two different, yet complementary, concepts to aid its diagnostics. The first, induction, provides the user with a decision tree resulting from the specified case and predefined aim (for example, identifying the faulty card in a system or detecting the fault in a card in a test). The second concept, Case-Based Reasoning, resolves thorny problems by using a set of similar cases as a guide in researching the fault.

Developed in two months, MET's application, which comprises today 300 different diagnostic cases, processes complex electronics cards for which the level of knowledge is low. The test equipment supplies information on the fault, which is displayed on the screen. Currently used on PCs, it will be transported soon to UNIX, the test equipment's operating system. Basing the system on UNIX allows technicians to use a single machine for testing and diagnostics, optimizing equipment use and repair time, since some diagnostics can be executed in the background of the test phase.

MET's first application aims to achieve ambitious objectives: Reducing overall diagnostic time by half while maintaining an accuracy rate of 70% and cutting rejects by 25%. The system allows the company to capitalize on the expertise and know-how of its technicians, and it allows them to multiply their talents and increase their knowledge.

For industrial uses, KATE's client-server architecture makes it an optimal solution for large-scale deployment. MET plans to extend the application to the detection of faulty electronics cards during final system tests.

## A.10   MÜRITZ ONLINE – Tourist Information on the Internet

*We notice more and more that customers utilize the Internet as their source of information. CBR-Works Online enables us to act as an information broker that satisfies this demand.*
Manfred Becker, Müritz Online

Müritz Online is a tourist information system on the Internet. It provides information on culture, nature, and leisure, and it offers available board and lodging possibilities in the Müritz, Germany, region. It was developed by tecInno together with Heinzel & Röhr GmbH & Co. KG using regio-tours online and CBR-Works. It aims at leveraging the local tourism industry.

The boarding assistant of Müritz Online gives you intelligent support during a search. Choose your hotel, bed and breakfast, or conference site in the region. Anyone can use it. Müritz Online demonstrates a surplus value that is a pre-requisite for the success of any system.

The success of this application is based on the added value for the tourist as compared to other media types. Travel services on the Internet are booming but do not offer much more than the usual catalogs of tourist companies. Müritz Online's boarding assistant demonstrates the real possibilities of an interactive-media Internet.

Müritz Online's surplus value to its users originates from the use of knowledge on geographical aspects and similarities among different types of boarding and leisure activities. It comprises improved search results, an increased comparability of different offers, and, in particular, a quick search success. For example, to find a comfortable hotel with a pool at a certain location, the user just describes his or her wishes. He may use one of three search modes: A quick search for basic information, an expert mode with all the details, or a sophisticated mode for conference sites. Based on its knowledge of boarding facilities and the region's geography, the system selects those offers that best meet his wishes. If there is no hotel with a pool, for instance, at the requested location, then a similar hotel within 2 kilometers will be proposed. By this intelligent search, the message "No entry found!" belongs in the past.

## A.11   ODENSE STEEL SHIPYARD – Improving Performances of Ship Welding Robots

*With the integration of KATE's CBR technology, and multimedia tools, we are able to reuse the knowledge of specialists and have our operators handle most maintenance tasks.*
Thomas Knudsen, Automation Development Department, Odense Steel Shipyard

Odense Steel Shipyard Ltd. (OSS) in Denmark is one of the market leaders in the design and building of large commercial ships. For more than a decade, it has increased performance and productivity by using huge robots that can weld 14 meters per hour. With 25 robots, OSS can weld more than 2.5 kilometers per day.

Consequently, reducing robot down-time is critical for the Danish shipbuilder. To that end, OSS launched a fault-diagnosis system development project in 1997 for its Multi-Robot Gantry System, the world's largest robot station. The station comprises 12 robot gantries located 17 meters above the shop floor. The robots are programmed off-line, and the station is scheduled by a shop floor control system. Four operators supervise the robots with the help of one maintenance technician.

The resulting diagnostic system, called Freya, was developed by a team of OSS maintenance specialists and operators in collaboration with KATE's editor AcknoSoft, Multicosm, the editor of a multimedia authoring tool, and experts from the Parallel Application Center. With Freya interfaced to the shop floor control system, operators are immediately aware of any robot malfunction, whereupon KATE searches approximately 500 cases, which describe possible robot faults and breakdowns, to give a diagnosis.

Freya's multimedia capability lets operators find not only technical documentation for robot maintenance, but mechanical and electronic drawings, pictures, and video clips. A sophisticated multilingual user interface allows operators in Odense to work in Danish, but the same system could be used by other OSS operators in Germany, France, Finland, or Norway, using their native language.

Built as a generic system, Freya is expected to be used for other robot stations and other types of equipment, such as cutting machines and cranes.

## A.12   SEPRO ROBOTIQUE – Customer Support of Robots for the Plastics Industry

*We had tried to build a rule-based expert system for over 6 months and had not obtained any convincing results. We were immediately impressed by the KATE approach and installed, in less than 6 months, a first version of a working system to improve our customer service support operations.*

Michel Jez, training division, Sepro Robotique

SEPRO manufactures robots that are used in the plastics industry. These robots manipulate plastic parts once the parts have been molded in an injection press. During the past 15 years, Sepro has sold more than 6,000 robots worldwide. Old models, which are no longer manufactured, are still in operation and must be supported. New technicians have no experience with old models: Turnover time for a service technician is about 4 years. The technicians must have competence in a wide range of domains, such as mechanics, hydraulics, electronics, and so on.

AcknoSoft's KATE was used to produce a troubleshooting system that is used by 8 help-desk technicians on a local network. It is connected to technical documentation and to a CAD system on a SUN workstation. The quality of the technical information (cases) is monitored by a steering committee, which includes staff from the customer support, training and engineering departments. Benefits of this intelligent help-desk are the following:

- it reduces the time to process a call, as well as the number of calls back,
- it reduces the number of wrong diagnoses
- it means field technicians are sent less often to the customer's site,
- it means the right spare parts are sent to the client,
- it decreases training costs;
- it builds a corporate memory of experience and preserves know-how about old robots.

A multilingual version of the system will be deployed worldwide at Sepro's locations.

## A.13   SEXTANT AVIONIQUE – Troubleshooting Avionics for Airbus Airplanes

*The main benefit of the CBR approach is that it capitalizes on the troubleshooting experience of skilled maintenance specialists so that the experience can be shared and transferred to novices.*
    Pierrick Noury, Technical Product Support Manager, Sextant Avionique

Sextant Avionique, a subsidiary of Thomson-CSF and Aérospatiale, designs and manufactures on-board electronics equipment used in planes and helicopters.

Looking for ways to improve its customer support and to reduce maintenance costs, Sextant Avionique's Civil Customer Support department has launched an innovative project that aims to reduce airplane downtime and minimize the number of "no fault found" by improving the quality of diagnosis.

While the information stored on Sextant Avionique's maintenance computer is very useful, it is not always sufficient to help the airlines and Sextant Avionique's maintenance engineers identify a faulty component.

A prototype of the diagnosis system has been developed for the Flight Management, Guidance and Envelope Computers (FMGEC) that equip all Airbus A330 and A340.

The system is presently available on a portable PC and may also become available on an Intranet. The diagnosis system was built with AcknoSoft's KATE, a data-mining tool that uses the power of Case-Based Reasoning technology. About 200 troubleshooting reports have been included in the prototype's database. CBR technology is used to find solutions to previously experienced incidents. It compares the current malfunction with ones that have already been solved, retrieves the most similar cases, and adapts the known solution to solve the current problem.

## A.14    SIEMENS – SIMATIC Knowledge Manager

*Because we provide up-to-date information about our products on our Internet server, we looked for a tool that would provide an easy-to-use user interface, high performance, and a high recall rate. Users of the system should not have to be experts on search engines. The only solution for this was a CBR system that has knowledge about our products and systems that users usually do not have. With our CBR application, both customers and internal engineers have instant access to this knowledge 24 hours a day and 365 days a year worldwide.*

Karl-Heinz Busch, SIMATIC Online Support, Siemens

Siemens A&D sells a wide range of industrial automation systems within its SIMATIC program worldwide. Subsidiaries of Siemens A&D, as well as other companies, are engaged in repairing and maintaining this equipment. Siemens A&D decided to use the World Wide Web to provide information, such as frequently asked questions or news about the latest products, via WWW pages. Because of the fast growth of this document collection, a simple folder-oriented categorization soon required a tremendous amount of maintenance and, at the same time, limited the benefit for users. Siemens also very soon realized that a standard information retrieval (IR) approach is not appropriate despite the availability of numerous tools. This is so for the following reasons:

— Products cannot be considered in isolation. Rather, relationships exist among the various products and components, which should be taken into account when searching for relevant documents. For example, the component $CP\ 1473$ $MAP$ is highly similar to another component named $CP\ 1430$. Also, some products are highly similar because they belong to the same series, whereas another group of products shows completely different properties. A wide range of such relationships exists, and demand is strong for a means of explicitly representing this type of knowledge.

— SIMATIC is not a single range of products but, rather, consists of more than a dozen different subprograms. Some of the products can be used for many programs, whereas others are highly specific for a single one. Again, this is a specific type of knowledge that somehow has to be represented in the CBR system.

The first versions of the Simatic Knowledge Manager (SKM), namely the Internet and Intranet versions, went online in March 1998; a first CD-ROM followed in April 1998. In December 1998, version 3.0 was delivered. The current version supports two languages, English and German. For both, the same knowledge model is used. This is possible because documents are represented by sets of concepts (e.g., products) that are independent of the underlying language. Besides the documents on the CD, this version also uses so-called *CD2Web* technology; if the user is online, it checks for up-to-date documents on the web and, thus, combines the advantages of both media: The fast access of the CD and the latest versions from the WWW. The CD-ROM contains about 26 MB textual data in approximately 3,500 HTML files per language. On the Internet, about 150 files are added per language per month. Internal users can access additional documents, so the volume of the database is approximately 80 MB in about 10,000 documents per language (as of December 1998). The use of the SKM on the CD cannot be measured yet, but use of the HTML version on the Internet server is promising. The number of sessions increased from 1,500 in August 1998 to 3,000 in November 1998, while during the same period the number of calls at the hotline remained the same.

## A.15   SNECMA   SERVICES  –  Troubleshooting   Boeing   737 Engines

*One of the main reason for selecting AcknoSoft's technology was the fact that KATE adopts the same reasoning process as would a maintenance specialist who discovers solutions from prior experience.*
    Richard Heider, Product Support, CFM International - Snecma Services

Snecma Services is a subsidiary of the engine manufacturer Snecma. Jointly with General Electric aircraft engines, Snecma has developed the CFM56-3 engine that equips all Boeing 737. To reduce maintenance costs, an innovative project called Cassiopee was launched. Troubleshooting represents about 50% of airplane downtime, and the main goal was to halve the time required for diagnosis, which means an overall reduction of 25% in downtime.

In 10 years, with over 80 million flight hours accumulated, 23,000 troubleshooting reports had been sent to the manufacturer by the airlines. Stored on an IBM mainframe, this reliability data was used as the starting point to build a PC-based diagnostic system using KATE. A first version of the system was developed in eight months.

However, the cases extracted from the raw data were incomplete, and as a consequence the diagnostics were fuzzy. The data was then sampled and the cases were reviewed by a maintenance engineer at the rate of 15 cases per hour. The system now contains about 1,500 "clean" cases. It uses a combination of CBR and fault trees, either the ones from the Boeing maintenance manual or decision trees generated by KATE-DataMining. CBR is then used to retrieve similar cases so that solutions to problems can be found faster than they would be by going through the steps of the manual, were some tests might be skipped. The system is linked to the illustrated spare parts catalog and to relevant electronics technical documentation. It enables airlines to share troubleshooting experience worldwide. As a manufacturer, Snecma can validate the technical content of the reported cases and update regularly the case base by means of CD-ROM.

Today Cassiopee is being tested by several large and small airlines throughout the world.

## A.16  THE COMPENDIUM "PRECISION FROM RHINE-LAND-PALATINATE" – Product and Catalog on the Internet

*By CBR-Works the user obtains a compass that easily guides him to the assets of the compendium.*
Prof. Dr. W. Ehrfeld, CEO of the Institute of Microtechnology Mainz (IMM)

The IMM is a center of excellence for microtechnology. Microtechnology plays a key role in the development of high-tech products and ordinary objects. It accelerates the advances in minimum invasive surgery, as well as in telecommunications. Other areas of application are new components and techniques for the automotive and aerospace industries. Microtechnology is a key technology for the next century. Additionally, the IMM hosts the European Contact Office of Rhineland-Palatinate and Hesse in Germany. It aims to strengthen collaboration and involvement of small- and medium-sized enterprises in the R&D programs of the European Union.

The Compendium "Precision from Rhineland-Palatinate" is a sort of Yellow Pages for high-tech purposes. If you are seeking specific manufacturing processes for certain materials, you can find them in this compendium on the Internet[2].

The compendium presents enterprises that offer services in the general area of high-precision tooling, including precision tooling, micro-tooling, precision optics, and electronics. If a specific service is unavailable in a region, e.g., flame-cutting, then CBR-Works offers a suitable nearby alternative, like plasma-cutting. The search for such suitable alternatives is based on the high precision know-how of the IMM.

This way the compendium provides access to the high-precision tooling competence of the IMM's experts for every interested party.

---

[2] http://www.imm-mainz.de

## A.17  WARTSILÄ NSD – Extending Marine Engine Life Cycles and Easing their Maintenance

*Some of our low-speed diesel engines are equipped with additional monitoring systems. These tools indicate the fitness of the engine, and permanent information of the engine operator is essential. Thanks to KATE, a failure in such a tool can be localized and repaired within a very short time, avoiding heavy and costly engine breakdown with less downtime.*

Karl Svimbersky, Head of the Engine Diagnosis Division, Wartsilä NSD

On a tanker, an engine breakdown can be catastrophic. First signs of such a breakdown call for rapid attention, but adequately qualified technicians are not always available on the high seas. Today, the main engine for a tanker costs between $6-$7 million, about 10% of the tanker's cost, and has a lifetime of 15 to 20 years. To guarantee an optimum life span, Wartsilä NSD has set out to provide onboard engine operators with as much assistance as possible.

Sensor-based operating systems continuously monitor the standard alarming system, mainly the piston's running behavior and its wear. They warn the operator before problems occur. But those surveillance systems themselves can break down without warning.

In 1996, Karl Svimbersky conducted a feasibility study that chose KATE's Case-Based Reasoning technology and charged AcknoSoft with developing a diagnostic system that could be used at sea. The pilot project focused on two of the most-sold monitoring tools of the Mapex product family. AcknoSoft created a case base from 120 carefully documented cases.

Now, when an engine operator at sea encounters a problem, he phones a technician in Winterthur (Switzerland). To get information on how to fix the current breakdown, the technician simply checks off a series of boxes on the screen. The diagnostic system then searches the case base for the previously solved problem that most closely matches the current case, and the system gives the technician precise repair instructions.

Today, the diagnostic tool is available on the workstations of Wartsilä NSD's maintenance staff. It will be deployed progressively onto their portables, with which they will be able to board a ship and access the engine's entire history, as well as data on previous repairs. Data captured on-board ship will be used to update the central case base.

Highly satisfied with the results of this project, Wartsilä NSD is studying the possibility of applying the technology to the entire maintenance process.

# Glossary

**Adaptation.** Adjusting a retrieved case to fit the given problem situation by applying *adaptation knowledge*.

**Adaptation Knowledge.** Adaptation knowledge is the expert domain knowledge about how to adapt a retrieved case from the case base so that it is better suited to the current problem. Adaptation knowledge is not mandatory for CBR applications but can be optionally used to improve the retrieved solutions.

**Agents.** In the INRECA methodology, agents are humans who enact a *method* in order to perform a certain *process*.

**Attribute-Value Pair.** A case can be represented as a flat set of attribute-value pairs where each pair encodes the value of a certain attribute for that case.

**Awareness.** The success of the project depends on all prospective users being made aware both of its implications and of the possibility that "there is something in it for them," thus generating motivation.

**Case.** A case represents one piece of reusable experience. Typically, a case consists of two parts: a problem description and a solution.

**Case Base.** This is the collection of all available cases.

**Case Base Administrator.** She/he has all rights over the system, including the right to update the domain model. Updating should be done occasionally as new experiences arise.

**Case-Based Reasoning.** Case-Based Reasoning (CBR) tries to model the acting by experience. It maintains a memory of experiences (*case base*) and solves new problems by *retrieving* similar cases from the cases.

**Case-Based Reasoning Cycle.** The CBR cycle describes the basic steps involved in case-based problem solving: *retrieve*, *reuse*, *revise*, and *retain*.

**Case Buffer.** This is a temporary location where current cases are stored pending a decision about whether or not to edit them into the case base.

**CASUEL.** CASUEL (Manago et al. 1994) is the object-oriented case representation language developed by INRECA. It allows the developer to define *domain models, cases, similarity measures,* and *adaptation knowledge.*

**Common Generic Level.** This is a level in the experience base of the INRECA methodology at which processes, products, and methods are collected that are common for a very large spectrum of different CBR applications.

**Conversational CBR Approach.** An approach to CBR in which a case is represented as a flat list of questions and answers, and the list of questions is different for every case; there is no *domain model.*

**Cookbook Level.** This is a level in the experience base of the INRECA methodology at which processes, products, and methods are tailored for a particular class of applications (e.g., help-desk, technical maintenance, product catalog). For each application class, the cookbook level contains a *recipe* (see below).

**Corporate Memory.** When corporate knowledge becomes easily retrievable for decision support, one speaks of a "corporate memory."

**CQL.** CQL is the case query language that is based on CASUEL. It is used to formulate queries to a CBR retrieval engine.

**Decision Tree.** This is one form of the output of an "induction engine." It displays successive partitions of a case base into subsets differentiated from each other by the values of parameters. The first parameter selected for the subdivision is the one generating the greatest information gain as regards factors leading to the target outcome. The subdivision process is then repeated for all other parameters within each branch. See also *fault tree.*

**Deployment.** When a system has been developed to the satisfaction of the users, it is usual to generate a "runtime version" of the software, in which all changes made to date are embedded robustly, and system users can use it without help from the developers. The system is then said to be "deployed."

**Domain Model.** In the *structural CBR approach,* the domain model is a set of attributes, with either defined sets of symbolic values or defined ranges of numerical values sufficient to characterize each unit of knowledge in the knowledge domain. Each case is represented using the attributes, each of which is given one of the allowed values.

**Experience Base.** The experience base is the collection of software development experience within the experience factory.

**Experience Factory.** An experience factory is a logical and/or physical organization that supports project development by analyzing and synthesizing all kinds of experience, by acting as a repository for such experience, and by supplying that experience to various projects on demand. An experience factory packages experience by building informal, formal, or schematized models.

**Fat Client.** When the CBR system is working in client-server mode, the master-version of the system resides on the server. However, for the system to work at an acceptable level of performance, a client with lots of computation capabilities might be necessary. This is called a "fat client," since it could require significant time to download to the client machine.

**Fault Tree.** A fault tree is a *decision tree* where the branches are based on the evidence leading to the diagnosis of a fault.

**GUI (Graphical User Interface).** The graphical user interface is usually customized interactively with the user to meet the user's needs. The information should be presented without overwhelming the user.

**Hierarchical Model.** Hierarchical models breakdown a complex system into a hierarchy of submodels, each of which has its own case base. A rule of thumb for the scale of a submodel is that it should have about 15 or so attributes.

**Induction.** Induction is the generation of rules or decision trees for achieving a desired outcome. The rules or decision trees are generated automatically from the analysis of cases in a case base. This induction process abstracts from the experience of many expert decisions stored as cases in the case base.

**Initial Domain.** This is a subset of the total target domain that is used in initial trials of the CBR approach. It should be selected so that positively perceived results are obtained rapidly, thus creating *awareness*.

**Integration.** Integration means bringing together the various parts of the CBR application: The search engine, GUIs, case base, related database, and so on.

**Knowledge Base.** Knowledge base is a generic word for an assembly of chunks of formally represented, distilled knowledge, some or all of which may be in the form of *cases*.

**Knowledge Container.** Knowledge container model, introduced by Michael Richter (see Richter 1998), describes the knowledge that a CBR system uses. The containers are the *vocabulary*, i.e., the *domain model*, the *case base*, the *similarity measure*, and the *adaptation knowledge*. In principle, each container could be used to represent most of the knowledge, but for efficient application development it must be carefully decided which knowledge to put into which container.

**Managerial Process.** The primary goal of managerial processes is to provide an environment and services so that software that meets the product requirements and project goals can be developed. The services enact the technical and the organizational processes.

**Method.** A method is a particular way of achieving a specific goal. A method can be simple or complex. In the latter case, it can embody a number of subprocesses and intermediate products.

**Methodology.** A methodology is a collection of methods and guidelines that enables a person to work effectively and efficiently in the domain for which the methodology has been developed.

**Nearest Neighbor Retrieval.** This is a search approach that selects experience based on some geometrical distance computed in the attribute space. The search engine evaluates the n-dimensional "distance" between the query and all cases in the case base, taking into account the weights. The results are presented in order of n-dimensional "proximity."

**Organizational Process.** Organizational processes cover those parts of the business process that need to be changed in order to make best use of a new software system. They address those parts of the user organization's business process in which the software system will be embedded. New processes have to be introduced into an existing business process, such as the training of end-users or the technical maintenance of the system. Existing processes may need to be changed or reorganized in order to make best use of the new software system.

**Precision.** This is the proportion of retrieved cases that turn out to be relevant to a user who needs specific knowledge.

**Process.** A process is an activity that has the goal of transforming some input product(s) into some output product(s). It is a clearly defined step in a development project.

**Process Input Product.** A process input product is a product that is consumed by a process in order to generate the desired output product.

**Process Model.** Process models identify and document the *processes*, *products*, and *methods* in a clear and understandable way. In the INRECA methodology, process models are used to document the experience stored in *cookbook-level recipes* and on the *common generic level*.

**Product.** A product is an object that is either consumed as input, modified, or created as output of a *process*. A "modified product" is a product that is changed during the enactment of a process. Typically, it existed before the process was executed. An output product is a product that is created as a result of the enactment of a process. This product did not exist before the process was executed.

**Project Plan.** The project plan is the temporal and logical sequence of processes that have to be executed and the products that have to be consumed, modified, and created to achieve the goal of the overall project.

**Recall.** This is the proportion of relevant cases from the cases base (in the context of the user's current knowledge need) that where retrieved by the retrieval engine.

**Recipe.** A recipe describes the processes used to build a CBR application for a particular application class. All recipes are collected in the cookbook level of the *experience base* of the INRECA methodology.

**Resources.** Resources are objects that might be required to achieve a project goal. They can be financial, temporal, or material, as well as human resources.

**Retain.** The retain phase is the fourth step in the *CBR cycle*. Retain means storing new experience in the case base.

**Retrieval.** The retrieval phase is the first step in the *CBR cycle*. Retrieval means selecting a relevant case from the case base. There are different techniques for retrieval, like traversing an induction tree or nearest neighbor retrieval.

**Retrieval Engine.** This is a software component that performs the retrieval, i.e., it selects a case from the case base.

**Reuse.** The reuse phase is the second step in the *CBR cycle*. Reuse is a synonym for "adaptation." It means modifying the retrieved case to fit the given problem situation.

**Revise.** The revise phase is the third step in the *CBR cycle*. During revision the proposed solution case is applied and evaluated in the business environment. If necessary, the proposed solution can be improved.

**Second-Level Support.** People in a company who have a greater depth of expertise than those in the "front office," who possess routine knowledge. Front-office people may have to refer problems to these experts.

**Similarity Measure.** A similarity measure is a computational function that computes the similarity between a case and a query. The similarity measure contains expert knowledge that evaluates whether a case contains information that is reusable in the current context defined by the query.

**Software Process Modeling.** Software process modeling defines what *processes* must be enacted and what *products* must consumed, modified, or created within a software project.

**Specific Project Level.** The specific project level describes experience in the context of a single, particular project. It contains project-specific information, such as a description of the particular *processes* that were carried out.

**Structural CBR Approach.** This is a CBR approach that relies on cases that are described with a set of predefined attributes. These attributes are described in a *domain model*.

**Technical Process.** Technical processes transform product information from the problem description to the final (software) system. They cover the development of the system and the required documentation itself.

**Textual CBR Approach.** In this CBR approach, cases are represented in free-text form. Keyword matching techniques are used for retrieval. There is no *domain model*.

**Tool**. A tool is a piece of software, or a hardware-software combination, used by an *agent* to enact a *process* according to a *method*.

**Vertical Platform.** A vertical platform is a collection of several preconfigured software components together with development guidelines (a *recipe* on the *cookbook level*) particularly tailored for a restricted application domain, such as a help-desk. It is often implemented using a general purpose CBR engine but incorporates domain-specific modifications.

# References

Aamodt, A. & Plaza, E. (1994). Casc-based reasoning: Foundational issues, methodological variations, and system approaches. *AI-Communications*, 7(1), 39-59.

Althoff, K.-D., Auriol, E., Barletta, R. & Manago, M. (1995). *A Review of Industrial Case-Based Reasoning Tools.* AI Perspectives Report, AI Intelligence, Oxford, UK.

Althoff, K.-D., Birk, A., Gresse von Wangenheim, C., & Tautz, C. (1998). CBR for experimental software engineering. In: M. Lenz, B. Bartsch-Spörl, H.-D. Burkhard, & S. Wess (Eds.). *Case-Based Reasoning Technology from Foundations to Applications*, Lecture Notes in Artificial Intelligence 1400, Chapter 9, Springer, 235-253.

Althoff, K.-D. & Wilke, W. (1997). Potential uses of case-based reasoning in the experience-based construction of software systems. In: R. Bergmann & W. Wilke (eds.), *Proceedings of the 5th German Workshop in Case-Based Reasoning (GWCBR'97)*, LSA-97-01E, Centre for Learning Systems and Applications (LSA), University of Kaiserslautern.

Basili, V. R., Caldiera, G. & Rombach, H. D. (1994). The experience factory. In: J. J. Marciniak (ed.), *Encyclopedia of Software Engineering*, Vol. 1, Wiley, New York, 469-476.

Bergmann, R., Breen, S., Fayol, E., Göker, M., Manago, M., Schumacher, J., Schmitt, S., Stahl, A., Wess, S. & Wilke, W. (1998). Collecting experience on the systematic development of CBR applications using the INRECA-II Methodology. In Smyth, B. & Cunningham, P. (Eds.) *Advances in Case-Based Reasoning (EWCBR'98)*, Lecture Notes in Artificial Intelligence, Springer, Berlin, Heidelberg, 460-470.

Bergmann, R. & Stahl, A. (1998). Similarity measures for object-oriented case representations. In Smyth, B. & Cunningham, P. (Eds.) *Advances in Case-Based Reasoning (EWCBR'98)*, Lecture Notes in Artificial Intelligence, Springer, Berlin, Heidelberg, 25-36.

Bergmann, R., Wilke, W., Althoff, K.-D., Breen, S. & Johnston, R. (1997). Ingredients for developing a case-based reasoning methodology. In: Bergmann, R. & Wilke, W. (Eds.) *Proceedings of the 5th German Workshop in Case-Based Reasoning (GWCBR'97)*, LSA-97-01E, Centre for Learning Systems and Applications (LSA), University of Kaiserslautern, 49-58.

Booch, G. (1994). *Object-oriented analysis and design. With applications.* Second Edition. Benjamin /Cummings Publishing Company.

Dellen, B., Maurer, F., Muench, J., & Verlage, M. (1997). Enriching software process support by knowledge-based techniques. In *Int. Journal of Software Engineering and Knowledge Engineering*, Vol. 7, No. 2, 185-215.

Heister, F. & Wilke, W. (1998). An architecture for maintaining case-based reasoning systems. In Smyth, B. & Cunningham, P. (Eds.) *Advances in Case-Based Reasoning (EWCBR'98)*, Lecture Notes in Artificial Intelligence, Springer, Berlin, Heidelberg, 221-232.

Leake, D. (1996). *Case-Based Reasoning: Experiences, Lessons, & Future Directions.* AAAI-Press.

Leake, D. & Wilson, D. (1998). Categorizing case-base maintenance: Dimensions and directions. In Smyth, B. & Cunningham, P. (Eds.) *Advances in Case-Based Reasoning (EWCBR'98)*, Lecture Notes in Artificial Intelligence, Springer, Berlin, Heidelberg, 196-207.

Lenz, M., Bartsch-Spörl, B., Burkhardt, H. D., & Wess, S. (Eds.). (1998). *Case-Based Reasoning Technology, From Foundations to Applications*, Lecture Notes in Artificial Intelligence, Vol. 1400, Springer, Berlin, Heidelberg.

Manago, M., Bergmann, R., & Wess, S. & Traphöner, R. (1994). CASUEL: A Common Case Representation Language - Version 2.0 ESPRIT-Project INRECA, Deliverable D1.

Neal, M. (1997). Parametric search: Evolving information retrieval for the Web. CADIS Inc. IDM v2n5 (Feb 29, 1997).

Racine, K. & Yang, Q. (1997). Maintaining unstructured case-bases. In Leake, B. & Plaza, E. (Eds.) *Case-Based Reasoning Research and Development* (ICCBR-97), Lecture Notes in Artificial Intelligence, Springer, Berlin, Heidelberg, 553-564.

Richter, M. (1998). Introduction. Chapter 1 in Lenz, M., Bartsch-Spörl, B., Burkhardt, H. D., & Wess, S. (Eds.), *Case-Based Reasoning Technology, From Foundations to Applications*, Lecture Notes in Artificial Intelligence, Vol. 1400, Springer, Berlin, Heidelberg, 1-15.

Rombach, H. D. & Verlage, M. (1995). Directions in software process research. In: M. V. Zelkowitz (Ed.), Advances in Computers, Vol. 41, Academic Press, 1-61.

Smyth, B. & McKenna, E. (1998). Modeling the competence of case bases. In Smyth, B. & Cunningham, P. (Eds.) *Advances in Case-Based Reasoning (EWCBR'98)*, Lecture Notes in Artificial Intelligence, Springer, Berlin, Heidelberg 208-220.

Stolpmann, M. & Wess, S. (1999). *Optimierung der Kundenbeziehungen mit CBR systemen-Intelligente Systeme für E-Commerce und Support,* Addison Wesley Longmann (Business & Computing), Bonn.

Surma, J. & Tyburcy, J. (1998). A Study on competence-preserving case replacing strategies in case-based reasoning. In Smyth, B. & Cunningham, P. (Eds.) *Advances in Case-Based Reasoning (EWCBR'98),* Lecture Notes in Artificial Intelligence, Springer, Berlin, Heidelberg, 233-238.

Thomas, H., Foil, R., & Dacus, J. (1997). New technology bliss and pain in a large customer service center. In Leake, B. & Plaza, E. (Eds.) *Case-Based Reasoning Research and Development* (ICCBR-97), Lecture Notes in Artificial Intelligence, Springer, Berlin, Heidelberg,, 166-177.

# Index

acquisition   114-120, 124-131, 139, 141, 150, 152, 162

Active Server Pages   139

adaptation   70, 115, 117, 118, 122, 123

administrative information   100, 103, 104

Adobe Acrobat   53, 138

agents   25, 67, 83-84, 92, 96, 99, 102

Analog Devices   4, 28, 35, 47-50, 55, 96, 136-138, 144, 160

Ansaldo   161-162

Ariane   162

attribute   21, 27-35, 39-44, 56-58, 116-117, 123, 134, 136, 141, 150-154

automotive   14, 163, 173

awareness creation   111-112

background knowledge   28, 31

banking   14

benefits   15, 49, 67-71, 74, 78, 109, 156

biology   14

business requirements   139-141

call center   25, 71, 73, 75

case acquisition   21, 40-44, 86, 114-120, 124, 126, 130-131, 139, 141, 150, 152, 162

case approval   44

case base editor   44

case base   11, 17-24, 29-48, 56-61, 68-76, 85, 115-126, 129-133, 138-143, 150-157, 164, 173

case buffer   41, 44, 122

case maintenance   44

case query language (CQL)   44

case structure   31, 33, 42, 135, 147

case   1, 2 10-48, 54-62, 68-78, 85-91, 114-156

Case-Based Reasoning   V-VII, 9-33

CASUEL   44, 141

catalog search   4, 18, 28, 35, 47-48, 66-67, 133-144, 161, 173

CBR consultant   113, 117

CBR cycle   71

CBR engine   28, 34, 143

CBR experience base   85, 106

CD-ROM   55, 69, 73, 85, 87, 92, 106, 127, 134, 138, 141, 161, 171, 173

CFM International   172

common generic level   86-92, 96

complex equipment   4, 72, 147, 148

complex method   84, 86, 94-98, 100, 103-105, 144

complex method description sheet   97, 103

conversational CBR   4, 19, 21-24, 25, 28, 34

cookbook level   86-88, 96, 109, 127, 131

corporate knowledge   9, 11, 15, 38, 66, 70, 76-77, 170

customer relationship management,
    V-VII, 9-10
customer service    10, 14, 62, 159,
    163, 169

DaimlerChrysler    2, 36-46, 130, 163
data mining    V-VII, 2, 9, 11, 14, 20-
    21, 162, 170
decision tree    10, 20, 25, 32, 172
deduction    14
development process    18, 49
diagnosis    119, 155, 164
domain model    17-45, 69-74, 84-85,
    104-105, 114-118, 124, 130,
    135-136, 140, 147-155
dynamic induction    20, 57, 59

electronics    14, 47, 62, 136, 149,
    167-173
embedded electronics    56, 59, 159-
    160
end-user    60-61, 110, 112, 116, 119,
    122, 135, 150
end-user training    111
evaluation    93-94, 119, 123, 126
experience base    80-92, 96-98, 105-
    106
experience factory    80-85
expert system    4, 16-17, 25, 39, 56,
    159, 169
expert users    114

fat client    43
fault    11-12, 18, 24, 34, 40, 57-59,
    118-119, 148-153
fault isolation manual    12
fault tree    59, 150, 153, 172
features    20-21, 27, 40, 45, 116, 137
first-level support    25, 36
frequently-asked questions    22, 23,
    70
Freya    169
front office    V, 9-10, 15

functional decomposition    151

generalization    14, 92
Gicep Electronique    164
goal definition    82, 111
graphical user interface    VI, 84, 92,
    96, 99 142, 143

health care    14
help-desk    4, 15-19, 35-47, 67, 85,
    93, 109-123, 129-133, 170
hierarchical data model    150-155
HOMER    4, 35-47, 109, 115-117,
    127-130, 163
hotline    22, 39, 47, 67, 163, 172
hotline operator    67
HTML    59, 61, 98-100, 105-106,
    139, 172

induction    11, 14, 20, 57, 59, 159,
    166, 167
information gain    42, 45
information management system    60
initial domain    30, 34, 111, 113
input product    83, 96, 98, 105
INRECA    1-4
INRECA methodology    VII, 1-4,
    11, 19, 63-157
integrated circuits    47, 160
integration    60, 116, 137, 142, 168
interfaces    61, 69, 74, 116, 139
Internet    VI, 4, 15-16, 31, 48, 60,
    69, 73-74, 97, 106, 134, 161,
    165-173
Irish Research Scientists Association
    (IRSA), 138, 144, 164
ISO 9000, 3, 79, 87

Java    41, 139

knowledge acquisition    39, 45-47,
    114-126

knowledge base    56, 66, 70, 76, 149, 159-162
knowledge container    117-126
knowledge management    71, 74-75, 112
knowledge repository    37-38, 46, 109-110, 113
knowledge utilization    120

Legrand    11, 165-166
line replaceable units    149

maintenance    VII, 12, 16, 21-46, 56, 59, 60-62, 69-70, 76, 79, 87, 90, 93, 109-131, 147-174
managerial processes    93, 111, 119
manufacturing    14, 16, 160, 166, 173
marketing automation    10
Matra Systems & Information    162
measures of success    66
method    83-84, 92, 94, 97-104
method description    100-104
method name    101, 104
methodology tool    4, 91, 104
mobile office    15
model hierarchy    57, 61, 151
model-based reasoning    56, 159
modified product    98
Multicosm    169

nearest neighbor retrieval    19
novice users    114

object structure    27, 136
Odense Steel Shipyard    168, 169
on-board computers    59
organizational process    93, 111-115, 120
organizational quality    112
output product    83, 92-98, 105

parametric search    17, 48-50, 55, 134-135, 160, 161, 165
precision    22, 35, 50, 160, 173
problem description    37-41, 46, 71-72, 118-121, 149, 151, 154, 162, 174
problem-solving    21, 36, 67, 110, 112, 116
process    80-84, 91-106,
process description sheet    97-98, 100-104
process goal    98
process model    36, 77, 80-95, 123, 126-129, 139, 151
process name    98
process quality    109, 112
product    80-84, 91-106
product description sheet    97, 100
product name    98, 100
project goal    93, 112-113, 119, 123
project management    79
project name    98, 100-101, 104-105
project plan    66, 79-95, 120, 123, 129, 156
project planning    80-81, 93, 95, 120, 123
project team    66, 111-126

quality control    18, 29, 33, 35, 79
quality improvement paradigm    80-83, 87, 91
quality standards    92
query    9, 17, 22, 28-31, 42-44, 50-53, 59, 134, 137

rapid prototype    114, 123, 126
recall    13, 22, 35, 171
recipe    87-91, 98-106, 109, 127-133, 139, 147, 155
recipe name    105
recycle    122
refine    48, 122-123, 134, 144, 151-152

reliability analysis    15
remedy    40, 119
requirements    47-50, 53, 67-69, 92-
    93, 96, 100, 115, 123-126, 133,
    135, 139-141, 160-161
resources    38, 83-84, 92, 95, 110-
    115, 127-130
retain    36-37, 122
retrieve    11, 17, 22, 28, 35, 36, 45,
    121, 172
reuse    3, 34-37, 47, 80-85, 90, 92,
    113, 116, 121-122, 129, 144,
    168
revise    36-37, 106, 121

sales    2, 4, 10-11, 15-16, 28, 47-50,
    67, 73-75, 135, 139, 140-141,
    160-161
sales automation    10
sales materials    139
sales support    15, 28, 160
savings    49, 55, 161, 163
search engine    49-50, 171
second level support    66
self-diagnostic    150
self-service    VI, 68, 70, 73-74
Sepro Robotique    27, 169-170
Sextant Avionique    170
Siemens    11, 171
SIMATIC Knowledge Manager    23,
    171
similaritiy    28, 34-35, 54, 69, 86,
    102, 117-118, 122-123, 133,
    137, 143, 168
simple method    84, 94, 97-105
simple method description sheet    97
smarter business decisions    2, 9-10
Snecma Services    172
software process modeling    80, 83,
    86, 91, 95
specific project level    86, 87, 89, 91
SPICE    3, 79, 87
statistics    4, 16

structural CBR    4, 21, 26-36,
subprocesses    84, 94, 98, 103, 104
system administrator    37, 44, 70
system development    111-115, 129
system guided dynamic induction    20
system implementation    111
system integration    111
system specification    111
system use    59, 111, 119-122, 128-
    131
system verification    111

technical equipment    109-110, 148-
    151
technical process    92-93, 110-115,
    120, 130
technical support    9, 11-12, 15, 18,
    48
telecommunications    14, 173
testing    12, 49, 71, 93, 115, 129,
    142, 144, 166-167
textual CBR    4, 21-23, 28, 34
TGV    4, 35, 56-62, 150-159
tool selection    113
transportation    14, 56, 62, 159
transportation market    56, 159
troubleshooting    68, 170, 172

unconfirmed case    122
user feedback    71-72
user guided dynamic induction    20
utilization process    111, 114

vertical platform    18-19, 135, 150
Visio    104-106
vocabulary    32, 114-123

Wartsilä NSD    174
Web interface    138-139
Web server    10, 41, 61
worldwide 24/7 support    73

XML    139

# Springer
# and the
# environment

At Springer we firmly believe that an international science publisher has a special obligation to the environment, and our corporate policies consistently reflect this conviction.

We also expect our business partners – paper mills, printers, packaging manufacturers, etc. – to commit themselves to using materials and production processes that do not harm the environment. The paper in this book is made from low- or no-chlorine pulp and is acid free, in conformance with international standards for paper permanency.

 Springer

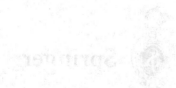

# Lecture Notes in Artificial Intelligence (LNAI)

Vol. 1476: J. Calmet, J. Plaza (Eds.), Artificial Intelligence and Symbolic Computation. Proceedings, 1998. XI, 309 pages. 1998.

Vol. 1480: F. Giunchiglia (Ed.), Artificial Intelligence: Methodology, Systems, and Applications. Proceedings, 1998. IX, 502 pages. 1998.

Vol. 1484: H. Coelho (Ed.), Progress in Artificial Intelligence – IBERAMIA 98. Proceedings, 1998. XIII, 421 pages. 1998.

Vol. 1488: B. Smyth, P. Cunningham (Eds.), Advances in Case-Based Reasoning. Proceedings, 1998. XI, 482 pages. 1998.

Vol. 1489: J. Dix, L. Fariñas del Cerro, U. Furbach (Eds.), Logics in Artificial Intelligence. Proceedings, 1998. X, 391 pages. 1998.

Vol. 1495: T. Andreasen, H. Christiansen, H.L. Larsen (Eds.), Flexible Query Answering Systems. Proceedings, 1998. IX, 393 pages. 1998.

Vol. 1501: M.M. Richter, C.H. Smith, R. Wiehagen, T. Zeugmann (Eds.), Algorithmic Learning Theory. Proceedings, 1998. XI, 439 pages. 1998.

Vol. 1502: G. Antoniou, J. Slaney (Eds.), Advanced Topics in Artificial Intelligence. Proceedings, 1998. XI, 333 pages. 1998.

Vol. 1504: O. Herzog, A. Günter (Eds.), KI-98: Advances in Artificial Intelligence. Proceedings, 1998. XI, 355 pages. 1998.

Vol. 1510: J.M. Zytkow, M. Quafafou (Eds.), Principles of Data Mining and Knowledge Discovery. Proceedings, 1998. XI, 482 pages. 1998.

Vol. 1515: F. Moreira de Oliveira (Ed.), Advances in Artificial Intelligence. Proceedings, 1998. X, 259 pages. 1998.

Vol. 1527: P. Baumgartner, Theory Reasoning in Connection Calculi. IX, 283 pages. 1999.

Vol. 1529: D. Farwell, L. Gerber, E. Hovy (Eds.), Machine Translation and the Information Soup. Proceedings, 1998. XIX, 532 pages. 1998.

Vol. 1531: H.-Y. Lee, H. Motoda (Eds.), PRICAI'98: Topics in Artificial Intelligence. XIX, 646 pages. 1998.

Vol. 1532: S. Arikawa, H. Motoda (Eds.), Discovery Science. Proceedings, 1998. XI, 456 pages. 1998.

Vol. 1534: J.S. Sichman, R. Conte, N. Gilbert (Eds.), Multi-Agent Systems and Agent-Based Simulation. Proceedings, 1998. VIII, 237 pages. 1998.

Vol. 1535: S. Ossowski, Co-ordination in Artificial Agent Societies. XVI, 221 pages. 1999.

Vol. 1537: N. Magnenat-Thalmann, D. Thalmann (Eds.), Modelling and Motion Capture Techniques for Virtual Environments. Proceedings, 1998. IX, 273 pages. 1998.

Vol. 1544: C. Zhang, D. Lukose (Eds.), Multi-Agent Systems. Proceedings, 1998. VII, 195 pages. 1998.

Vol. 1545: A. Birk, J. Demiris (Eds.), Learning Robots. Proceedings, 1996. IX, 188 pages. 1998.

Vol. 1555: J.P. Müller, M.P. Singh, A.S. Rao (Eds.), Intelligent Agents V. Proceedings, 1998. XXIV, 455 pages. 1999.

Vol. 1562: C.L. Nehaniv (Ed.), Computation for Metaphors, Analogy, and Agents. X, 389 pages. 1999.

Vol. 1570: F. Puppe (Ed.), XPS-99: Knowledge-Based Systems. VIII, 227 pages. 1999.

Vol. 1571: P. Noriega, C. Sierra (Eds.), Agent Mediated Electronic Commerce. Proceedings, 1998. IX, 207 pages. 1999.

Vol. 1572: P. Fischer, H.U. Simon (Eds.), Computational Learning Theory. Proceedings, 1999. X, 301 pages. 1999.

Vol. 1574: N. Zhong, L. Zhou (Eds.), Methodologies for Knowledge Discovery and Data Mining. Proceedings, 1999. XV, 533 pages. 1999.

Vol. 1582: A. Lecomte, F. Lamarche, G. Perrier (Eds.), Logical Aspects of Computational Linguistics. Proceedings, 1997. XI, 251 pages. 1999.

Vol. 1585: B. McKay, X. Yao, C.S. Newton, J.-H. Kim, T. Furuhashi (Eds.), Simulated Evolution and Learning. Proceedings, 1998. XIII, 472 pages. 1999.

Vol. 1599: T. Ishida (Ed.), Multiagent Platforms. Proceedings, 1998. VIII, 187 pages. 1999.

Vol. 1609: Z. W. Raś, A. Skowron (Eds.), Foundations of Intelligent Systems. Proceedings, 1999. XII, 676 pages. 1999.

Vol. 1611: I. Imam, Y. Kodratoff, A. El-Dessouki, M. Ali (Eds.), Multiple Approaches to Intelligent Systems. Proceedings, 1999. XIX, 899 pages. 1999.

Vol. 1612: R. Bergmann, S. Breen, M. Göker, M. Manago, S. Wess, Developing Industrial Case-Based Reasoning Applications. XX, 188 pages. 1999.

Vol. 1617: N.V. Murray (Ed.), Automated Reasoning with Analytic Tableaux and Related Methods. Proceedings, 1999. X, 325 pages. 1999.

Vol. 1620: W. Horn, Y. Shahar, G. Lindberg, S. Andreassen, J. Wyatt (Eds.), Artificial Intelligence in Medicine. Proceedings, 1999. XIII, 454 pages. 1999.

Vol. 1621: D. Fensel, R. Studer (Eds.), Knowledge Acquisition Modeling and Management. Proceedings, 1999. XI, 404 pages. 1999.

Vol. 1634: S. Džeroski, P. Flach (Eds.), Inductive Logic Programming. Proceedings, 1999. VIII, 303 pages. 1999.

# Lecture Notes in Computer Science

Vol. 1585: B. McKay, X. Yao, C.S. Newton, J.-H. Kim, T. Furuhashi (Eds.), Simulated Evolution and Learning. Proceedings, 1998. XIII, 472 pages. 1999. (Subseries LNAI).

Vol. 1586: J. Rolim et al. (Eds.), Parallel and Distributed Processing. Proceedings, 1999. XVII, 1443 pages. 1999.

Vol. 1587: J. Pieprzyk, R. Safavi-Naini, J. Seberry (Eds.), Information Security and Privacy. Proceedings, 1999. XI, 327 pages. 1999.

Vol. 1590: P. Atzeni, A. Mendelzon, G. Mecca (Eds.), The World Wide Web and Databases. Proceedings, 1998. VIII, 213 pages. 1999.

Vol. 1592: J. Stern (Ed.), Advances in Cryptology – EUROCRYPT '99. Proceedings, 1999. XII, 475 pages. 1999.

Vol. 1593: P. Sloot, M. Bubak, A. Hoekstra, B. Hertzberger (Eds.), High-Performance Computing and Networking. Proceedings, 1999. XXIII, 1318 pages. 1999.

Vol. 1594: P. Ciancarini, A.L. Wolf (Eds.), Coordination Languages and Models. Proceedings, 1999. IX, 420 pages. 1999.

Vol. 1596: R. Poli, H.-M. Voigt, S. Cagnoni, D. Corne, G.D. Smith, T.C. Fogarty (Eds.), Evolutionary Image Analysis, Signal Processing and Telecommunications. Proceedings, 1999. X, 225 pages. 1999.

Vol. 1597: H. Zuidweg, M. Campolargo, J. Delgado, A. Mullery (Eds.), Intelligence in Services and Networks. Proceedings, 1999. XII, 552 pages. 1999.

Vol. 1598: R. Poli, P. Nordin, W.B. Langdon, T.C. Fogarty (Eds.), Genetic Programming. Proceedings, 1999. X, 283 pages. 1999.

Vol. 1599: T. Ishida (Ed.), Multiagent Platforms. Proceedings, 1998. VIII, 187 pages. 1999. (Subseries LNAI).

Vol. 1601: J.-P. Katoen (Ed.), Formal Methods for Real-Time and Probabilistic Systems. Proceedings, 1999. X, 355 pages. 1999.

Vol. 1602: A. Sivasubramaniam, M. Lauria (Eds.), Network-Based Parallel Computing. Proceedings, 1999. VIII, 225 pages. 1999.

Vol. 1603: V. Vitek, C.D. Jensen (Eds.), Secure Internet Programming. X, 501 pages. 1999.

Vol. 1605: J. Billington, M. Diaz, G. Rozenberg (Eds.), Application of Petri Nets to Communication Networks. IX, 303 pages. 1999.

Vol. 1606: J. Mira, J.V. Sánchez-Andrés (Eds.), Foundations and Tools for Neural Modeling. Proceedings, Vol. I, 1999. XXIII, 865 pages. 1999.

Vol. 1607: J. Mira, J.V. Sánchez-Andrés (Eds.), Engineering Applications of Bio-Inspired Artificial Neural Networks. Proceedings, Vol. II, 1999. XXIII, 907 pages. 1999.

Vol. 1609: Z. W. Raś, A. Skowron (Eds.), Foundations of Intelligent Systems. Proceedings, 1999. XII, 676 pages. 1999. (Subseries LNAI).

Vol. 1610: G. Cornuéjols, R.E. Burkard, G.J. Woeginger (Eds.), Integer Programming and Combinatorial Optimization. Proceedings, 1999. IX, 453 pages. 1999.

Vol. 1611: I. Imam, Y. Kodratoff, A. El-Dessouki, M. Ali (Eds.), Multiple Approaches to Intelligent Systems. Proceedings, 1999. XIX, 899 pages. 1999. (Subseries LNAI).

Vol. 1612: R. Bergmann, S. Breen, M. Göker, M. Manago, S. Wess, Developing Industrial Case-Based Reasoning Applications. XX, 188 pages. 1999. (Subseries LNAI).

Vol. 1614: D.P. Huijsmans, A.W.M. Smeulders (Eds.), Visual Information and Information Systems. Proceedings, 1999. XVII, 827 pages. 1999.

Vol. 1615: C. Polychronopoulos, K. Joe, A. Fukuda, S. Tomita (Eds.), High Performance Computing. Proceedings, 1999. XIV, 408 pages. 1999.

Vol. 1617: N.V. Murray (Ed.), Automated Reasoning with Analytic Tableaux and Related Methods. Proceedings, 1999. X, 325 pages. 1999. (Subseries LNAI).

Vol. 1620: W. Horn, Y. Shahar, G. Lindberg, S. Andreassen, J. Wyatt (Eds.), Artificial Intelligence in Medicine. Proceedings, 1999. XIII, 454 pages. 1999. (Subseries LNAI).

Vol. 1621: D. Fensel, R. Studer (Eds.), Knowledge Acquisition Modeling and Management. Proceedings, 1999. XI, 404 pages. 1999. (Subseries LNAI).

Vol. 1622: M. González Harbour, J.A. de la Puente (Eds.), Reliable Software Technologies – Ada-Europe'99. Proceedings, 1999. XIII, 451 pages. 1999.

Vol. 1625: B. Reusch (Ed.), Computational Intelligence. Proceedings, 1999. XIV, 710 pages. 1999.

Vol. 1626: M. Jarke, A. Oberweis (Eds.), Advanced Information Systems Engineering. Proceedings, 1999. XIV, 478 pages. 1999.

Vol. 1628: R. Guerraoui (Ed.), ECOOP'99 - Object-Orinted Programming. Proceedings, 1999. XIII, 529 pages. 1999.

Vol. 1629: H. Leopold, N. García (Eds.), Multimedia Applications, Services and Techniques - ECMAST'99. Proceedings, 1999. XV, 574 pages. 1999.

Vol. 1634: S. Džeroski, P. Flach (Eds.), Inductive Logic Programming. Proceedings, 1999. VIII, 303 pages. 1999. (Subseries LNAI).

Vol. 1639: S. Donatelli, J. Kleijn (Eds.), Application and Theory of Petri Nets 1999. Proceedings, 1999. VIII, 425 pages. 1999.